ANDRÁS LÁSZLÓ

SOLUM IPSUM
METAPHYSICAL APHORISMS

Middle Europe Books
Budapest
2024

Originally published in Hungarian as
Solum Ipsum. Metafzikai aforizmák © Kötet
English translation © HyperBoar
Collected, edited, & afterword by Ferenc Buji
Foreword by Róbert Horváth

English text revised by Miklós Taliga & Viktória Vukics
Edited by András Vukics

Hardcover ISBN: 978-1-64264-189-9
Paperback ISBN: 978-1-64264-190-5
E-book ISBN: 978-1-64264-191-2

This translation is a substantial revision of the previous English translation by Andrea Gál, Gábor Horváth, Mónika Parragh, & László Virág, and was made by András Vukics.

Layout by Greg Johnson. Translation edited by John Morgan. Index by James O'Meara. Cover by Kevin I. Slaughter. Cover photograph by Géza Péter Nagy

Abyssus abyssum invocat

Contents

Foreword ◆ 9

The Aphorisms ◆ 11

Prologue ◆ 13
Weltanschauung & World-Contemplation ◆ 13
Metaphysica Fundamentalis ◆ 18
God ◆ 22
The Universal Subject ◆ 23
Auton & Heteron ◆ 24
Subject & Object ◆ 25
The Magical Nature of the Being ◆ 27
Person & Subject ◆ 28
Man ◆ 30
Conduct of Life ◆ 31
Metaphysical Praxis I: Attitude ◆ 38
Metaphysical Praxis II: The Principles ◆ 41
Metaphysical Praxis III: The Concretes ◆ 46
Master & Disciple ◆ 48
Metaphysical Realization ◆ 49
Tradition & Anti-tradition ◆ 54
Anti-traditional Forces ◆ 56
The Dark Age ◆ 59
Postmodernity ◆ 68
Perspectives of the Future ◆ 69
Spiritual Deviation—Spiritual Deceit ◆ 71
Nature & the Supra-Natural ◆ 75
Humanism ◆ 75
Materialism ◆ 76

Objectivism ◆ 78
Politics ◆ 78
Egalitarianism—Democracy—Liberalism ◆ 85
From Supra-historicity to Sub-historicity ◆ 90
Culture ◆ 92
Art & Beauty ◆ 96
Science ◆ 97
Religion ◆ 98
Christianity ◆ 101
Philosophy ◆ 102
Ethics ◆ 103
Symbology ◆ 104
Evolution & Involution—Progress & Decline ◆ 105
Woman—Matrimony—Family ◆ 107
The Sacred & Profane Aspect of Sexuality ◆ 108
Combat—War—Heroism ◆ 112
Thinking & Intuition ◆ 113
Feeling & Emotion ◆ 115
Cognition ◆ 116
Hierarchy ◆ 117
Quantity & Quality ◆ 119
Body—Soul—Spirit ◆ 120
Death & Immortality ◆ 122
Eschatology ◆ 126
The Beginning & the End ◆ 127
Domination (Dominatio) & Power (Potestas) ◆ 129
Time & Eternity ◆ 131
Order ◆ 134
Freedom ◆ 135
Epilogue ◆ 136

Afterword ✦ 139

András László & metaphysical traditionality ✦ 139
Traditionality versus Modernity ✦ 140
András László ✦ 147
Solipsism—Kali-Yuga—Rightism ✦ 150

Index ✦ 175

About András László ✦ 197

Foreword

The metaphysical "aphorisms" in the present volume have been taken from from András László's oral teachings. András László is as famous an author in Hungary as René Guénon and Julius Evola are in Europe, or Frithjof Schuon is in the United States. But for those who know him well, his personality and attitudes also exhibit characteristics that are identical to those of authentic Eastern spiritual masters. (Of course, this statement does not intend to suggest that Guénon, Evola, and Schuon did not themselves possess traits that are characteristic of spiritual masters.)

András László has never claimed to be a *guru*. His personality and spiritual function are instead reminiscent of those of the *ācāryas* (*mahācāryas*).

It goes without saying that in today's West, even authentic spiritual teachers cannot assert themselves in the same way as did, for example, Bhagavān Śrī Ramaṇa Maharṣi in his time and place. We have no churchly buildings teeming with spiritual life, or spiritual centers where we can meet physically—and if somehow we are yet granted such facilities, they often merely serve to distance the seekers from themselves and from the essence of the spiritual teachings. We are forced to meet in the streets and in cafés, subject to forms that are mostly distasteful to us, and that can be said to be anything but pure or ideal.

But these circumstances and forms—no matter how deep their impact—are irrelevant. What is essential is perennial wisdom, which can be known, preserved, and realized independently of time and space.

These teachings of András László were selected—with the author's approval and with minimal corrections—by one of his former disciples, Ferenc Buji. This volume therefore contains those aspects of László's teachings that preoccupied Buji—an excellent editor and talented author in his own right—and that he regarded as most important, especially those teachings relating to the *kali-yuga*. That said, the work he has done is invaluable.

Róbert Horváth
Budapest, September 8, 2004

The Aphorisms

Prologue

1 ✦ Just as the Buddha said: "I speak unto them whose eyes are covered but with slight dust"—covered, but only slightly. That is, he speaks neither unto them whose eyes are completely covered with dust, nor unto them whose eyes are not covered at all.

Weltanschauung & World-Contemplation

2 ✦ Only those may reject something with validity who are at the same time able to defend it fully, and only those may advocate something with validity who are at the same time able to refute it fully.

3 ✦ A Weltanschauung, whether it is adequate or inadequate, is the product of decline.

4 ✦ Concerning every evil, it should be supposed that it might be good, and concerning every good, it should be supposed that it might be evil.

5 ✦ If someone is unable to overcome his own upbringing and the influences he was subjected to at home, at school, or by mass communication, then how could he conceivably overcome those obstacles which will arise as ontic bondage along his spiritual way?

6 ✦ To eliminate defective valuations, one should carry out a radical self-correction in the course of which one's *every* former view must be rejected, whereupon those that pass the test of being measured against one's new viewpoint should be embraced anew.

7 ♦ Just as the notion that stealing apples is inappropriate entails that stealing pears is also inappropriate, so too does the judicious man need to be advised only concerning a few points in order to correct certain substantial elements in his views, so that at other such points he may make the corrections himself.

8 ♦ Changing one's Being- and world-concept is not enough; this is a mere prerequisite for something much more important: the transmutation of the Being- and world-*contemplation*.

9 ♦ Not only a view but a way of seeing; not only a view of the world but viewing the world; no mere worldview but world-contemplation; not merely structure and a framework but a living process...

10 ♦ Whatever Weltanschauung one attributes to oneself is important, but only of secondary importance. It is important because the spiritually-oriented man will obviously not define himself as a materialist. In spite of this, however, one may still be deeply materialistic as regards one's essential nature. Views are very important, but viewing, seeing, and contemplation are even more important, and if *these* remain materialistic—that is, if one's very cogitation, despite one's professed doctrines, retains the primary characteristics of the materialistic concept both functionally and substantially—then whatever one may call oneself, one remains a materialist.

11 ♦ The existence of a Weltanschauung guarantees the presence of principles; the presence of contemplation corrects the Weltanschauung.

12 ♦ A genuinely valid concept is valid not because it offers a better description of reality, but in that it directs attention to the fact that judgments have consequences that do not remain on the level of mere description.

13 ♦ The description of Being in metaphysical traditions is only apparently a description of Being, and the aim of such a description of Being is only seemingly descriptive. The true aim is consequential and normative: consequential because the description entails consequences with respect to realization; and normative because it relates to the norms of realization. Thus if I assert, for example, that God is not subject to the laws of logic, I thereby declare that my aim is to transcend the laws of logic.

14 ♦ Correct views, if half-accepted, are always worse than the most incorrect views thoroughly professed.

15 ♦ There is nothing more dangerous than the almost perfect.

16 ♦ Concepts that are almost perfect are far more dangerous than those that are entirely unacceptable.

17 ♦ The prevailing worldview of the present age is worldviewlessness, and the various particular worldviews are superimposed on this platform with the aim of further deepening the worldviewlessness.

18 ✦ The less one has views and the more one has personal interests, the more one is inclined to regard one's interests as views.

19 ✦ The "ideal" of the dark tendencies is the man without worldviews.

20 ✦ The reason why man lies to himself is that *mentally* he is unable to bear what *existentially* he tolerates all the more easily: that he is unworthy enough not to even have views. But the time is not far off when he will be able to mentally accommodate his unworthiness as well.

21 ✦ False rhetoric: "The truth of solipsism is the highest truth—but there is one truth even beyond this: the Lamb of God."

22 ✦ In false rhetoric, even the false rhetor does not believe in what he says, though he would willingly sacrifice his very life for it—and even then he would still not believe in it.

23 ✦ (The false rhetor) He knows his rhetoric is not true, but he would like it to be true. Yet he himself does not know why.

24 ✦ If the distinction between the primary, the secondary, and the tertiary fades away, then the complete worldview blurs; and someone whose worldview, *Weltanschauung*, and world-contemplation become blurred cannot possibly attain the uttermost essence of his self.

25 ✦ It is true that the modern *view* is dangerous, but the modern *function* is even more dangerous.

26 ♦ "Incoherence, incompetence, inconsequence" (Carl Kerényi): this is the fundamental spiritual attitude of the second half of the twentieth century.

27 ♦ A terminological error is never merely a terminological error.

28 ♦ Each and every modern worldview has the role of attacking man's psycho-spiritual organism at a given specific point.

29 ♦ In the background of the modern world's conceptions, elaborated by a vast rational apparatus, manias are operating which are generated by demonic forces.

30 ♦ If the cosmic concept lacks hypercosmic centrality, then the cosmic concept becomes one oriented towards chaos. Without *hypercosmia*, the cosmos is doomed to destruction—because the cosmic character of the cosmos, that is, the orderliness of the cosmos—derives from a hypercosmic center.

31 ♦ Those concepts wherein God is present not in an integral way, penetrating every element and the whole structure, but to which spirituality is, as it were, only attached from the outside, should be treated with the utmost reservation. A genuinely spiritual concept should be spiritual *in its every particle*.[1]

---

[1] Typical examples of this type of false concept are the theologies of Pierre Teilhard de Chardin and Karl Barth.

32 ♦ Spiritual and theistic worldviews in every area of life—in eating, sleeping, walking—but more importantly in their views should be markedly different from the materialistic and atheistic concept.

33 ♦ The fact that a worldview is universal does not mean that it is universally homogeneous, but that it is universal and differentiated, both in its aspect and according to hierarchical levels.

34 ♦ Among the plurality of schools, metaphysical traditionality is the only one which pays attention to both that which is extra- and super-temporal, and that which is the consequence of the temporal present. While the goal is atemporally eternal, the condition of man from whence he can set off towards this goal is continually shifting.

35 ♦ Every stance in connection with metaphysics is a stance through which man declares his own state of self-experience.

36 ♦ Metaphysical traditionality is the only concept almost *crying out for* realization.

METAPHYSICA FUNDAMENTALIS

37 ♦ In fact, nothing can be said about metaphysics. One can only speak about it for the sake of realization.

38 ♦ Metaphysics is the path whereby I travel through myself.

39 ♦ There is but one true normality: the normality of the center.

40 ♦ If knowledge connected to the center is lacking, then there is in fact no knowledge of the periphery, either.

41 ♦ What relates to becoming can only be interpreted from a point that is above becoming.

42 ♦ The "metaphysical" is not simply the highest step in a flight of stairs; the "metaphysical" is realized by breaking out of the circle of beings.

43 ♦ Metaphysics differs from religion by virtue of the fact that, by turning towards the Subject, the latter says "Thou," while the former says "I."

44 ♦ Taken in the most universal sense, nothing can be propounded outside consciousness; in fact, outside consciousness—to use an only apparently double negative formulation—even the *nothing* can*not* be propounded.

45 ♦ That which is completely "immanent" is the same as that which is completely transcendent.

46 ♦ The only manifested thing is the Unmanifested—which, while manifesting Itself, remains yet unmanifested.

47 ♦ In its origin and root, every fallen state of the Being is the Subject's free act in the spiritual sphere.

48 ♦ Every manifestation is at the same time a descent.

49 ✦ The principle that "as above, so below" is perfectly true—but only when viewed from above.

50 ✦ *Saṁsāra* and *nirvāṇa* are one—but only when viewed from *nirvāṇa*.

51 ✦ All beings *are* simultaneously on all existential planes: they are present both in the center and at the periphery of the Being.

52 ✦ Beyond a certain level, there is no external or internal anymore. There is no such thing as external or internal—because relative to the limits of consciousness, everything is inside; while relative to the center of consciousness, everything is outside.

53 ✦ Existential planes are not actual conditions, but levels of intensity of the metaphysical vision (Sanskrit *vidyā*).

54 ✦ An Idea is an intuition of myself by myself according to an existential modality.

55 ✦ States of the Being are nothing but states of self-identification.

56 ✦ The wisdom of non-differentiation is superior to the wisdom of differentiation, but it cannot be achieved without the wisdom of differentiation. Therefore, the wisdom of non-differentiation must be preceded by the wisdom of differentiation.

57 ✦ I can unite only that which I have previously separated.

58 ✦ Amalgamation is the most extreme antithesis of unity.

59 ✦ An experienced thing implies and presupposes the experience itself; experience implies and presupposes the experiencer.

60 ✦ The experiencer, the process of experiencing, and the experienced can be differentiated and should be differentiated—but they cannot be disrupted. For independently of any experiencer there can be no experiencing, and independently of any experiencing nothing can be experienced.

61 ✦ Polarity—in close connection with axiality and centrality—always signifies that the whirlpool of the Being does not touch the origin of that which penetrates into the earthly-human world. Polarity is the expression of the celestial, extra-*saṁsāra*ic origin.

62 ✦ The Earth can only essentially be in touch with Heaven (the Unmoved Mover) only where it is not in motion—i.e., at the poles.

63 ✦ The Idea of a thing is not an infinitely subtle entity somewhere, but something within the metaphysical vision.

64 ✦ In the world, the spirit manifests as light. When Christ says, "I am the light of the world,"[2] it means that He is the light of that world that is beyond the world—that is, He is the spirit of the world, but this spirit is beyond the world.

---

[2] Cf. John 8:12: "I am the light of the world."

65 ♦ The material world is essentially a spiritual world. What does "spiritual" mean? Does it mean that it is subtler than the material? It does, but this is not the main point. The world is spiritual only if its conscious nature becomes an experienced reality.

66 ♦ The whole Being is conscious.

God

67 ♦ Of only one thing can it be said that it is impossible for it not to exist, and the existence of only one thing is an absolute certainty and an apodictic necessity (*necessarium apodicticum*): the existence of that which is actually above existence.

68 ♦ "To be"—this expression can only be applied analogically to the *Metaphysicum Absolutum*.

69 ♦ If I say that God "exists," then I take God as an ideal objectivity; that is, I desacralize Him—and this is blasphemy.

70 ♦ If God were outside me, then God would be one of the things that exists and not God. Propounding an objective God is in fact an indirect denial of God.

71 ♦ Strictly speaking, we cannot say whether God exists or not. God is what He is only through realization; otherwise He is a possibility: the possibility of Myself. In a sense, God does not exist, but "may exist."

72 ✦ God creates *out of* Himself, *within* Himself, and *into* Himself: *into the interior* of Himself.

73 ✦ Not only may God do anything (*omnipotentia*), but He also does do everything (*omniagentia*).

74 ✦ God is infinitely beautiful because He infinitely resembles Himself.

75 ✦ God's omnipresence does not primarily mean that He is in everything and that He pervades everything, but rather that everything resides in God.

THE UNIVERSAL SUBJECT

76 ✦ There is but one subject and that subject is I myself.

77 ✦ After I have distinguished (Sanskrit *viveka*) and separated (Middle High German *Abegeschiedenheit*) everything from Myself, it becomes clear that everything is Myself.

78 ✦ Everything that exists is an illusion. The only thing that is not an illusion is who/what I am.

79 ✦ The "is-ness" of the Subject is so certain because it is beyond is-ness. What is in the sphere of is-ness can never be certain in the sense of infinity.

80 ✦ Strictly speaking, an abstract universal Subject would be an abstract universal Object.

81 ♦ There are two possible cardinal errors relating to solipsism: one is to speak about *ātmā*, that is, the true Self as if it were an abstract object; the other is to identify the absolute Subject with my given and definite personal being.[3]

82 ♦ Giving up even a morsel of solipsism is equivalent to giving up all of it.[4]

Auton & Heteron

83 ♦ Every *heteron* ("other") is non-recognized *auton* ("myself").

84 ♦ The extraneous *auton* is no *auton*—it is *heteron*. It behaves like the *auton*, yet there is a fundamental difference between them: while that *is*, I *am*.

85 ♦ The name of the recognized Subject is *auton*, "myself"; the non-recognized Subject's name is *heteron*, "other." The *heteron* is *auton* as well, but non-recognized *auton*.

---

[3] Metaphysical solipsism—according to the Latin terms *solum* ("solely") and *ipsum* ("myself")—asserts that the Being has but one subject, and that—putting it in first person singular (for this is the only way to formulate it)—is I myself: I myself not as a person, however (for there are infinite persons), but as the universal Subject which is the root and source of the person. For more details, see the Epilogue.

[4] That is, between solipsism and subjective idealism the distance is greater than between subjective idealism and materialism—just as between the highest level of the world of Becoming and the *Metaphysicum Absolutum* the ontic distance is much greater than between the lowest and highest levels of the world of Becoming.

86 ♦ The *heteron* is illusory not because it does not exist, but because I do not grasp it as I should actually grasp it: as myself.

87 ♦ The world exists so that I can reintegrate it into myself. Or, according to a different interpretation but with the same meaning: it exists so that I can separate it from myself: the world *qua* world, *qua heteron* to separate it from myself, and the world *qua* potential *auton* to reintegrate it into myself.

88 ♦ The entire external world is *heteron*, but inactive *heteron* and hence not dangerous. On the contrary, what is truly dangerous is the inner *heteron*, because the inner *heteron* is active.[5]

89 ♦ Perceiving the *heteron* in its totality—that is, not only as a *datum* but together with its *datatio* and *dator*—is equivalent to perceiving the *heteron* as myself.

90 ♦ The perfect *heteron* is nothingness.

SUBJECT & OBJECT

91 ♦ The object implies the action, and the action implies the subject, for the action derives from the subject and the object derives from the action.

92 ♦ Every objectivity is the objectivity of consciousness.

---

[5] The inner *heteron*—active but imperceptible, or perceptible only through its effects—is for example the hidden subject of rambling thoughts and emotions.

93 ♦ As consciousness has subjective reality (consciousness itself), and as consciousness has actional realities (the faculties of consciousness), so has consciousness *within* consciousness objective reality: the entire objective world itself.

94 ♦ It is evident that there is objective reality; calling it into question would be senseless. But to assert that this objective reality can be independent of consciousness—*of my consciousness*—is totally unfounded, because objective reality is the objective reality of the very consciousness, of the very subject.

95 ♦ The world does not exist as an objective reality existing independently of consciousness, but as something that is dependent on consciousness. Indeed, not only is there a reality that is dependent on consciousness, but it is a reality that inseparably belongs to consciousness: it is indeed "of consciousness." As regards its substance, the world is a coagulated reality of consciousness: it is in consciousness and consists of consciousness.

96 ♦ As the dream state is an objective reality of the dreaming consciousness, so is the waking world the objective reality of the waking consciousness. Both are objective realities—and both objective realities depend on the corresponding consciousness.

97 ♦ The unity of subject and object must be realized—but it is important how we attain this unity. If it is attained in the object, the result is nothingness. If it is attained in action, it will result in floating in an illusory equilibrium which cannot result in perfection because a movement towards either the object or the subject will eventually bring it to an end.

The unity of object, action, and the subject must be realized *within the subject*.

98 ♦ I am always more than what I can see. Indeed, I am always more even than what I suppose.

THE MAGICAL NATURE OF THE BEING

99 ♦ Reality—an illusion; but a real illusion.

100 ♦ *Māyā* does not mean that something conceals something, and that reality is under a veil. *Māyā* means that the *entire Being* comes into being in a state of enchantment, and when the spell is broken, the entities will not remain in their enchanted state.

101 ♦ In every perception—using first person singular—*I am* the creator. Who else could it be?

102 ♦ "It exists even if I do not experience it, because when I slept the world did not cease to exist"—so says the naïve realist. But how does he know this? Through being told by others when he woke up. But if one is living in an overall dream, then certain dream images might carry weight in some respect, but by no means in the sphere of ontological considerations.

103 ♦ Creatorness is magic and createdness is also magic—only in a different sense: creatorness is the magic of the magus, the enchantment of the enchanter, but createdness is the magic of the enchanted one.

104 ♦ Even in the most enchanted being there is something of the magician—hence it may reduce itself to the all-preceding and all-surpassing position of the magician.⁶

PERSON & SUBJECT

105 ♦ The fundamental alienation, the fundamental decline is the personality itself: this is when I alienate myself from myself.

106 ♦ Personality means that I am not perfectly myself, but only *secundum quid,* only according to something am I myself; but I want *secundum se,* that is, to be myself according to myself.

107 ♦ The Being cannot have several subjects, but only one, and this subject can only be I myself.

108 ♦ There cannot be so superior a spiritual vision wherein someone else's subjective nature can be revealed. For the Subject is not present in someone else; the Subject is present in me. I am allowed to speak about someone else as a subject-bearer only when I experience him as myself.

109 ♦ I may be able to perceive the soul or even the spirit in someone else. But I cannot perceive the Subject in anyone else, because the Subject is only in me.

---

⁶ "Reduce" is here used in the alchemical sense of the Latin *reducere, reductio* (to lead back), that has no connotation of diminishment—rather on the contrary. (Translator's note)

Person & Subject

110 ♦ The Subject is always, I am.

111 ♦ Man is a subject-bearer—but not merely in the sense that every being is a subject-bearer. In man's consciousness, his self manifests from the infinity behind his personality: his self as Subject.[7]

112 ♦ The Subject manifests constantly in a person, and there is no distance between the two; yet between the person and the Subject lies the entire cosmos and the totality of beings, which separates them by wedging in between them.

113 ♦ The person is one of the Subject's identification points: what I experience *in concreto*.

114 ♦ In my actual condition I am not the absolute as Myself, but already in my actual condition am I myself present in the absolute sense.

115 ♦ The *person*, the mask (Latin *persona*), in fact conceals the Subject—but at the same time, in the sense of a unique aspectual self-revelation, it manifests It as well.

116 ♦ In the actual "myselfness," it is always "myselfness" projected into "non-myselfness" that I experience.

117 ♦ The person is the starting point of the path leading back to Myself.

---

[7] But this of course becomes a perfected reality only if the *heteron* appears as *auton* in self-experience.

Man

118 ♦ Man in the highest degree and as a first step *creates* his incarnation; then, descending lower, he *chooses* it; descending even lower, he freely *accepts* it; descending yet lower, he *involuntary takes notice* of it: perhaps he would like to avoid it, but he cannot any longer. Descending even lower than this degree, he *encounters* it; and finally, he unconsciously *falls into* his incarnation—into the very incarnation that was originally freely created by himself.

119 ♦ Createdness—especially in its lowest degree, which corresponds to *creatio factiva* and the latter's most external state—means that I do not experience myself either as the creator of myself, or as the creator of my own faculties, or as the creator of my own world. Strictly speaking, creatureness is equivalent to obscuring my own nature as a creator.

120 ♦ Each and every man is a versional incarnation of the Universal Man.

121 ♦ The cherub who expelled man from Eden is that former rank of man which keeps guard over the Edenic state of being. And from this point of view, man was expelled by man from Paradise—which essentially means: I myself expelled myself from myself.

122 ♦ Contemporary man—and the man of any era whatsoever—is nothing but an identification.

123 ♦ Man never—not even in the deepest states of enchantment—regards himself merely and exclusively as one of the beings.

124 ♦ Every mask (*persona*) conceals a face (*facies*).

125 ♦ Not only does man carry his ancestors in himself, but he represents them as well.

126 ♦ The personal man experiences himself almost as if he existed in the third person singular.

127 ♦ Psychological I-ness is not the *awareness* of I-myself-ness, but a *feeling* of the I-ness.

128 ♦ The unconscious is potential consciousness.

129 ♦ If a man intends to place himself in the physical world or understand himself biologically, then this can be of some significance from a certain point of view, but from the point of view of realization, it can only serve to further alienate myself from myself.

130 ♦ While there are extreme divergences between people in terms of intelligence, as regards sensory perception, everyone—with only slight differences—is equally "stupid."

131 ♦ The darkness carried within man represents a heteronomy that is more extreme than any other darkness.

CONDUCT OF LIFE

132 ♦ Life is a spiritual challenge.

133 ♦ The aim of man's activity in life can either be the absolute or nothingness.

134 ♦ Between people, exomorphological differences are already quite significant; but endomorphological differences can be quite extreme as well.

135 ♦ That which is created is important; the process of creation is more important; but the most important is the creator.[8]

136 ♦ All kinds of confusion in principles is at the same time a confusion of identity.

137 ♦ When the essence is ignored, what happens is not only that what is most important is missing, but that the vacuum left by the essence is then filled by something else.

138 ♦ Sticking to the merely-human leads not to remaining on the human plane, but to becoming subhuman. For persisting in something is the same as losing it: losing that very thing that one wanted to retain.

139 ♦ The one in whom the problems of life, consciousness, and death do not arise cannot in the strictest sense of the word be regarded as a human being. He undoubtedly looks like a man, but in reality he is not.

140 ♦ If it is not through supra-human principles that man intends to change himself, then he will not remain in a human state but descend into a subhuman condition.

---

[8] It is the created that is often called creation—quite erroneously.

141 ♦ He who is without any goals beyond life is not only following a wrong path, but in the strict sense he should not even be called human.

142 ♦ He who is not able to live his life as a constant ascension culminating in perfection in the period right before death, but who instead begins to decline after reaching a certain age, in fact *abuses* his life.

143 ♦ He who does not strive upwards, sinks downwards.

144 ♦ He who lets himself be taken by the current is certain to follow the wrong path.

145 ♦ Today, even stagnation requires exceptional effort.

146 ♦ Every stagnation sooner or later turns to regression, decline, or descent.

147 ♦ In those who experience stagnation in life, descent has already begun, even if it is not so remarkable as to be immediately noticeable.

148 ♦ A striking sign of stagnation is when one procrastinates instead of attending to his spiritual tasks.

149 ♦ There are periods in one's life when the likelihood of a halt and of foundering is especially great. For the majority it happens around the age of twenty-seven—that is, between the age of twenty-four and thirty. This is when one maintains that "his world-concept has taken shape" by then. Of course this does not mean that it has taken shape, but rather that it has terminated halfway. Concerning those

with really insignificant spiritual qualifications, this usually happens between the age of fifteen and twenty-one. It is a considerable achievement, as it were, if someone founders only between the age of thirty-three and thirty-nine.

150 ♦ Upon developing completely, most people begin to decline straightaway—not only somatically, but in inner aspects as well.

151 ♦ Most people are infantile until about the midpoint of their lives, that is, until the age of thirty-six; immediately after that they grow senile from one day to another.

152 ♦ The majority of people are not mediocre, for true mediocrity is well above the average. The so-called average man is feeble *in all respects*: the forces of darkness are just as feeble in him as are the forces of light.

153 ♦ The lives of people in general fail as a result of mediocre conditions, and not because of the most negative conditions—since everyone resists the latter to some extent. But against mediocre conditions, the overwhelming majority of people are helpless: for these are not bad enough that they will revolt against them, yet just bad enough to impede spiritual development.

154 ♦ Consciousness is active, creative, and cognitive *comprehension*.

155 ♦ The reason why one should read is in fact to have the opportunity to think, and the opportunity to understand. For when I understand, I am more than human. When I understand, I am myself.

156 ♦ In understanding, *I myself* understand—and this is its true value: that *I* understand. True, it is not without significance *what* I understand; but the essence is that *I* understand.

157 ♦ Everything can be faked: even miracles, and indeed the very awakening; only one thing cannot be: intelligence.

158 ♦ Anything can be done to a man—he can even be turned into a frog—save for one thing: he cannot be made superior.

159 ♦ A truly intelligent man cannot be devoted to destructive ideas—for such an orientation always signifies some kind of mental disorder.

160 ♦ He who wants to be the mover cannot be the moved. He who wants to stop, cannot be stopped.

161 ♦ Even if shackled in the external sense, one is in no graver bondage than when he is fettered by his own inner darkness.

162 ♦ In the final analysis, man is not subjected to external factors but to his inner psychological states.

163 ♦ What manifests as democracy in the world is equivalent to automatisms, whirling associations, distraction, and lack of self-control in dominating the circus of consciousness.

164 ♦ Each and every individual-personal mania is a usurper, and each and every mania represents the terroristic aspect of the usurped power.

165 ♦ The truly negative in someone's ravings is not that he is raving, but that it is not in fact even he who is raving, but rather something or someone within him.

166 ♦ Not only does he sin who commits a crime by losing his self-control, but also he who, through a lack of self-control, does nothing.

167 ♦ He who does good on a sudden impulse in fact sins.[9]

168 ♦ In he who allows instincts to play an extranormal role, that which is realized is not freedom but rather the rule of instincts—*over himself*.

169 ♦ If ever there was an action without as much as a trace of autonomous will, it is the very one performed under the aegis of "I do whatever I want."

170 ♦ The fact that man in "self-feeling" experiences himself to some extent in the third person singular is manifested most clearly when he feels sorry for himself.

171 ♦ If someone is selfish, in fact he is not selfish in favor of himself, but in favor of that other for whom he mistakes himself, and to whom he wants to give advantages.

172 ♦ If there is some truth in the statement that "when mourning for someone, one in fact feels sorry for himself,"

---

[9] "Since, according to the traditional view, there is no greater sin than loss of self-control, in the Eastern traditional world a premeditated crime was judged as less grave than if committed on sudden impulse" (András László).

then no less true is the statement that when one is feeling sorry for himself, one is in fact feeling sorry for someone else.

173 ♦ "Everyone strives for good, but without finally reaching it," they say. But perhaps they do not reach it because they are not aiming for it ... Perhaps everyone indeed reaches his goal after all ...

174 ♦ Without exception, everyone reaches his goal, if they *really* have this goal.

175 ♦ Man is always born in the place where he has to be born.

176 ♦ Man should arrange his external world always so that it correspond to his internal world.

177 ♦ Between man's inner world and the surrounding vast and chaotic world, there is a definite correspondence.

178 ♦ All that is somatic in man—that is, which is in connection with body and face—mainly expresses the past.

179 ♦ Resignation to one's fate and revolt against one's fate are both lunar attitudes. The truly spiritual attitude aims at transcending fate: one is neither resigned or revolts against it, but by depriving fate of its importance, transcends it.

180 ♦ A first-rate man seeks the company of first-rate men. A second-rate man that of the third-rate.

181 ♦ It is always the inferior who disturbs the superior with his activity. It is always the superior who disturbs the inferior with his existence.

182 ♦ One should in fact only keep in contact with such people who open upward-pointing paths for one's life.

183 ♦ Modesty is just as much a sign of deviation as is arrogance.

184 ♦ No doubt, respect is almost extinct in today's children. But has there remained so much as a morsel of respectability in today's adults?

185 ♦ There is nothing respectable in adults, but even if there were, children would not respect them; and if children did respect adults for some reason, that would not make the adults any more respectable. It is not that one causes the other, but both share a common root. The world deteriorates starting from shared points.

186 ♦ From a spiritual perspective, humor is indispensable, and jokes are permissible, but making fun of something—especially in connection with higher realities—is unacceptable.

METAPHYSICAL PRAXIS I: ATTITUDE

187 ♦ Metaphysical doctrines are intended for those who are, in an existential sense, *at the crossroads*. This does not necessarily mean a strained situation, but rather a range of possibilities wherein a considerable number of people

Metaphysical Praxis I: Attitude

abide. Yet, the overwhelming majority of people eventually choose a downward path—not necessarily consciously, but for example by putting off one's inner transmutational measures: "I shall concern myself with this later."

188 ✦ As for metaphysical realization, every "must" concerns only the one who intends to do something with oneself. He who does not intend to do anything with himself, does not *need* to do anything.

189 ✦ In the past, metaphysical realization required only the will for realization. Later, realization necessitated initiation as well. Even later, initiation already presupposed preparation. While today, even the preparation of preparation is necessary, and indeed, an all-preceding self-correction as well.

190 ✦ In times past, a single school, a single sacred book, even a single sentence from such a book was sufficient: through it, everything could be achieved. Today, if one wants to return to the spirit, one has to surround himself with a multitude of traditions, schools, and currents.

191 ✦ Even two thousand years ago, the spiritual path was designated the "narrow path," or was compared to the edge of a sword. This path is, however, not simply narrow, but is also becoming *increasingly* narrower and more impassable, too. The "wide path," on the other hand, which lots of people tread in relative happiness, is actually a wayless path: a wide path, which is not even a real path—because it leads *nowhere*, to nothingness, to death...

192 ✦ The return to the origin is no one's fate or condition: it is beyond the context of fate, beyond all spheres of conditions.

193 ✦ It is never the circumstances that are really decisive.

194 ✦ Whatever a man wants to reach he reaches. If it should not happen, it is because he is *unable* to want it.

195 ✦ He who wants to awake, awakes.

196 ✦ The reason why someone does not become an initiate is never that he is not able to find an appropriate initiatory center, but that he is not mature enough for initiation.

197 ✦ Man can go through his life in such a way that he honestly says to himself and to others that his goal is this and that, while his goal is absolutely not that, but something totally different.

198 ✦ That which is spiritually positive is completely removed from the purpose of providing a comforting harbor for various psychic defects.

199 ✦ Spiritual paths are no paths for the psychically ill, for fugitives, for those who long for safety because they could not find it in their lives. Spiritual realization is a path for the sovereign type of man.

METAPHYSICAL PRAXIS II: THE PRINCIPLES

200 ✦ I cannot get anywhere else other than where I have already been—for where I have been, there I potentially *am*.

201 ✦ If the primary and ultimate Center were not always present, it would never be possible to reach it.

202 ✦ Only those can rise who are essentially up high.

203 ✦ Every true ascent from below is an ascent driven from above. The reason why I aspire for the higher is that the higher in me "calls" what is lower in me.

204 ✦ The adequate and legitimate way of returning to Heaven is symbolized by Jacob's ladder: reaching Heaven is only possible by climbing the ladder which descends from Heaven. The inadequate and illegitimate way is the story of the Tower of Babel: the ascent from the Earth necessarily leads to collapse and confusion.

205 ✦ The ultimate goal is the reduction from personal identification to absolute identification.

206 ✦ To take a step towards oneself, one must take this step within oneself. And to take steps toward others, one must previously have taken these steps within oneself as well.

207 ✦ To reach what is beyond and above the person, to the Subject transcending and essentially preceding the person, I cannot get to It in any other way but through the person, and only from my identification with the person can

I reduce myself, through myself, to my ultimate, primary, all-preceding, and all-crowning Self.

208 ♦ He who seeks the Origin and Goal anywhere other than within himself will never find It even in a theoretical sense. In him who finds the Origin and Goal within himself in a theoretical sense, the intention of realization may arise: to lead the consciousness back to the Center, whence it originates, and wherein it has its completion.

209 ♦ There is no goal whatsoever, unless I designate the goal within myself; there is no starting point whatsoever, unless I designate the starting point within myself; and there is no path whatsoever, unless I tread the path myself within myself.

210 ♦ In reducing myself into my own self, that is, into my ultimate goal, I transform myself from creature into creator.

211 ♦ The Subject cannot possibly be aimed at in an outward direction. I can only reach the Subject through my personal consciousness.

212 ♦ In the course of true spiritual realization, the object of the inner spiritual experience is of tertiary importance (all false teachings regard it as primary); the secondary is the action and course of experiencing; and the primary is the experiencer himself.

213 ♦ The more superior an experience is, the more the experience itself and the experienced itself get reduced and integrated into the experiencer.

214 ♦ As in the course of becoming, *svadharma*, leading from the supra-personal towards the person, made the person *qua* person possible, so also, in the course of realization, it is the *svadharma* that leads the person towards the supra-personal.[10]

215 ♦ *Svadharma*, one's own law, not only implies what a man should do in the world, and in what way he should lead and organize his life; *svadharma* is also the path that, when found and followed, enables one to return to Oneself.

216 ♦ The spiritual man is spiritual not because he is interested in spiritual matters—though no doubt, every spiritual man is interested in spirituality. The spiritual man is spiritual because he models his life in accordance with the order of the spirit, and leads it guided by the presence of the spirit.

217 ♦ That which does not lead not back towards the Center leads towards the periphery.

218 ♦ He who wants the Goal should also want the means that lead to the Goal, for if he does not want the means leading to the Goal, he certainly does not want the Goal.

219 ♦ According to the traditional view, every state one reaches or fails to reach is a question of power or powerlessness.

---

[10] The Sanskrit *svadharma* designates the law pertaining specifically to a given individual.

220 ♦ The more a creature is a creature, the frailer he is, the more corruptible, the more subject to circumstances, the more confined to the sphere of attractions and repulsions.

221 ♦ It is not the objectivities appearing objectively, but the objectivities which never appear objectively, namely the inexperiencable *heterons*, that represent the most powerful and dangerous forces leading one astray.

222 ♦ The power that fundamentally influences the quality of being, as my own power, cannot awaken while I myself am subject to attractions and repulsions.

223 ♦ Spiritual arousal and spiritual motivation necessitate that there be no nook in life left out of the transformation demanded by the spirit. There is no such thing as "I do it on Sunday, but don't do it on Monday." There is no separate domain. Neither is it a separate place where one takes off or puts on one's hat.

224 ♦ No asylum should be granted for darkness within one's life.

225 ♦ In order to fulfill the very high requirement of "Know thyself!," man should first but study himself—with cool neutrality and intensive interest.

226 ♦ He who is incapable of engrossment is not capable of doing anything serious.

227 ♦ Spiritual conduct of life is inconceivable without strict rhythmicity.

Metaphysical Praxis II: The Principles

228 ♦ Every spiritually positive deed, action, and operation arises from a specific adequate mixture of spontaneity and intentionality.

229 ♦ The *sine qua non* of all spiritual progress is extended intellectual interest.

230 ♦ On the spiritual path, various obstacles might arise, but there is only one absolute obstacle: stupidity.

231 ♦ Inner processes cannot be willed in such a vulgar way as when one wills oneself to push an enormous wheelbarrow.

232 ♦ The spiritual man should on the one hand put some distance between himself and the modern world, and on the other he should oppose it as a markedly anti-traditional world.

233 ♦ From *kali-yuga*—not the historical one, but *kali-yuga* in the essential sense—there is no awakening. Only from the Golden Age might there be an awakening.[11]

234 ♦ Why did Jesus Christ ascend to Heaven from the top of a mountain? Not because Heaven was nearer from there. Ascension from a mountain symbolizes that from the general levels of the Earth, there is no reaching Heaven. Only a

---

[11] According to Hindu doctrine, *kali-yuga* is the last, darkest—that is, the least penetrated by the spiritual—and at the same time the shortest period of the quaternary cosmic era. For more about *kali-yuga*, cf. the aphorisms under the heading "The Dark Age" and the Afterword.

point emerging from the Earth can be an adequate starting point of Heavenly ascension.

235 ♦ Modern man is uninitiable—but this does not mean that it is impossible to initiate a contemporary man.[12]

236 ♦ The initiate, in his own inner world, differs as much from a non-initiate as man differs from an animal.[13]

237 ♦ No one can be effectively coerced towards the spirit.

METAPHYSICAL PRAXIS III: THE CONCRETES

238 ♦ In every manifested state, it is essential that one should swim against the current towards the source.

239 ♦ To swim against the current, backwards, towards the Source, towards the Light, towards God, towards Myself...

240 ♦ It is impossible to initiate modern man—only archaic man can be initiated. Therefore man's task above all is to archaize himself.

241 ♦ Descent, the "going down to the netherworld," should occur by all means, and indeed, it does occur by all means,

---

[12] That is, not every contemporary man can be considered modern, for while contemporaneity is a chronological category, modernity is an attitude.

[13] A general traditional teaching, known almost everywhere. The initiate is of course not yet awakened. The degree of initiatedness corresponds approximately to the degree of salvation. In this connection, cf. the 259th aphorism.

and intentionally. But while my descent through my own volition will be followed by ascent, if I descend upon yielding to the forces of an extraneous will, then this descent will not be followed by ascent.

242 ♦ Realization without asceticism is pure nonsense.

243 ♦ He who rules over himself, rules over the world.

244 ♦ Through achieving mastery over consciousness, mastery over the Being is achieved, too.

245 ♦ While I am unable to control my circumstances, I should at least try not to allow circumstances to rule over me.

246 ♦ What detaches *bandha* (bondage) from *karma* (action), and what disallows action on the level of deed to become fate, is nothing other than control.[14]

247 ♦ The most fundamental question, the "Who am I?" formulated by Ramaṇa Maharṣi with a concentrative-meditative-contemplative aim—is in fact a question which cannot be answered in the sense of a formulation. The question of "Who am I?" is a question, but not in the same sense as questions are questions. "Who am I?" is the key sentence of my travelling through myself formulated as a question: verbally still a question, but inwardly not.

---

[14] This is the principle of *karma-yoga*. What binds one is not the very action, but uncontrolled action—that is, action wherein the subject of the action is not maximally present.

248 ♦ It is possible to fix one's attention on anything, but to concentrate (Sanskrit *dhāraṇā*) is possible only on an intuition, or at least the scent of a recently-departed intuition.

249 ♦ To attempt self-correction in the domain of unrealizable tasks is an excellent opportunity to *avoid* correcting oneself.

250 ♦ There is hardly a better chance to exempt oneself from the requirements of realization than by setting such high norms for oneself as are surely unattainable.

251 ♦ Making haste is from the devil, but so is procrastination.

252 ♦ *Ahogy Lehet*: only this remains open for contemporary man.[15]

Master & Disciple

253 ♦ The *ācārya*, the *guru*, and the *buddha* have in fact but a single absolute and inalienable attribute: no matter what form he manifests in, with his work he never increases darkness.

254 ♦ "Once the disciple has matured, the master will appear," they say in India. We would rather put it this way: He who has matured will dream the *ācārya* into his own dream of Being.

---

[15] *Ahogy Lehet* (i.e. "as it is possible") is the title of a Hungarian Catholic journal published in Paris.

255 ♦ The source from whence one learns something only seemingly provides any justification; in fact, it justifies nothing. If someone *really* knows something, then it is entirely irrelevant whether he heard it on a tram or learned it from an Eastern master.

256 ♦ He who cannot find the disciple within himself cannot find the *guru* within himself, either.

METAPHYSICAL REALIZATION

257 ♦ Mere subsistence is no state of realization. He who *finds* himself subsisting within life, *loses* himself in death.

258 ♦ Realizing myself is equivalent to creating myself: to become the cause and author—that is, the ruler—of my own being.

259 ♦ The ultimate goal is salvation—but beyond the ultimate goal there is yet another goal, an absolute goal: the awakening. Any goal is a goal only in this sense: any goal is a goal only because this absolute goal *exists*—since without an absolute goal, there could be no relative goals, either.

260 ♦ There is no cosmic level relative to which there is no higher, cosmic level. And there is no cosmic level relative to which there could not be a lower cosmic level. Wandering in the cosmos can be endless—and this is exactly why metaphysical realization is not a further piling up of levels, but an absolute dimensional breakthrough.

261 ♦ Realization takes place along the very same route as becoming took place—only in reverse.

262 ♦ Only that can be realized which has never ceased to exist.

263 ♦ It is not something situated somewhere that should be experienced, be it close or far; it is *myself* that I should experience, that which is here—but free from any personal or cosmic limitations.

264 ♦ The Goal, which is in the infinite, is forever present.

265 ♦ To be infinitely Myself: this is the Goal.

266 ♦ Realization is the realization of myself as the Absolutum.

267 ♦ Man's real task is to transmute himself from *individuum isolatum* into *Individuum Absolutum*.

268 ♦ The goal is to get from identification to attain the autonomous identifier. This is the goal—the goal which determines the path and determines the starting point, and in which it turns out that the goal and the starting point are in fact one.

269 ♦ If I transform myself totally into Myself, all the powers reigning over me cease. The dethronement of the "other" reigning over me means that I deprive myself, as non-recognized myself, of sovereignty, and enthrone Myself recognized as Myself. For recognizing Myself is equivalent to realizing Myself; and realizing Myself is equivalent to being free and sovereign.

270 ♦ Yoga is realization: absolute Self-realization; a Self-realization that takes man out of the human world, out of the world of becoming, and along a path that he has opened up within himself that leads to the Center of the Being which is beyond Being.

271 ♦ To awaken is the same as awakening Myself, for although I am Myself in every moment, I am not yet Myself absolutely. I myself transforming myself through myself totally to myself: this is the awakening.

272 ♦ Realization means the realization of the unity of object and subject. If, however, this unity is attained in the object, it is equivalent to the destruction of the individual. Through realization, the unity in the subject should be attained.

273 ♦ In realization, I should reduce myself from objects towards actions and from actions towards the subject; in the opposite direction the essence is never to be found—unless I recognize myself in what exists. For in the object *qua* object, the essence is never to be found; but in the object *qua* the subject manifesting through actions, it is possible that it can be found.

274 ♦ Total realization is the unity of the Center and the periphery.

275 ♦ Absolution is not a private achievement. Awakening is the awakening of *the Being*.

276 ♦ Through the awakening of man, the whole world awakens.¹⁶

277 ♦ In restoring myself, I restore the world.

278 ♦ He who becomes a *buddha* realizes the totality of the Being.

279 ♦ Yoga is a way through which I gain power *to make* Being.

280 ♦ Absolute Self-realization is the absolute realization of the Being wherein it comes to light that I, atemporally, am the creator, sustainer, and transmuter of the Being.

281 ♦ *Nirvāṇa* is nothing other than the *deflammatio* of the "other."¹⁷

282 ♦ *Nirvāṇa* is neither in a concrete nor in a figurative sense a place somewhere awaiting one's arrival. In fact, *nirvāṇa* cannot be entered as we enter a room. It is realized by and with my entering it. In any case, it is the same in our most ordinary everyday life as well...

283 ♦ Man does have a cosmic task, but his ultimate goal lies beyond the cosmos. This ultimate, absolute goal beyond

---

¹⁶ Just as in the case of ordinary dreaming, through the dreamer's awakening his whole dream-world awakens, integrating back into the very dreamer.

¹⁷ "*Deflammatio*" is András László's Latin-based neologism referring to a flame flaring up one last time just before it goes out. Thus, it means both flaring-up and a fading-out (extinction) at the same time.

Metaphysical Realization

the cosmos is nowhere else but *here*—but between my *hic et nunc* personality that is in the cosmos and my *hic et nunc* subjectness beyond the cosmos, there lies everything: Heaven, Hell, and Purgatory; the Worlds, the Chaos, and the Cosmos.

284 ✦ Metaphysical realization is ultimately open to every man, but this does not at all mean that everybody is fit for it. Only those are fit for metaphysical realization who represent the ascending and upward-striving aspect of the unique, Universal Man.[18]

285 ✦ In theory, the path of realization is open to every man, since almost directly behind and above the person stands the Subject; in practice, though, only the elite of the spiritual elite have a chance for realization, for in between the person and the Subject, the totality of existence, the whole cosmos lies.

286 ✦ Incapacity for realization can first and foremost always be attributed to a lack of *pistis*.

287 ✦ The fear of annihilation is only a secondary arch-fear; the primary arch-fear is the fear of awakening.

288 ✦ In the process of realization, even descent can have its own place, provided it is under control.

289 ✦ Realization and what is realized in realization is not a reward, but an achievement.

---

[18] For—according to the 120th aphorism—each and every man is a versional incarnation of the Universal Man.

290 ♦ Every being awakens—but not according to its own identification.[19]

Tradition & Anti-tradition

291 ♦ Tradition is a handing over (Latin *trans-dare*): the handing over of a supra-temporal set of principles within time.

292 ♦ Tradition is the atemporal thrown into temporality.

293 ♦ Knowledge of the origin, knowledge of the path, knowledge of the ultimate, all-transcending goal: this is metaphysical tradition.

294 ♦ Tradition derives from the eternal, points to the eternal, and represents aspiration towards the eternal in the human form of being.

295 ♦ Metaphysical tradition is at the same time solar and polar: polar, for though appearing in the earthly-human world, it is of heavenly origin, and for this reason its origin is unaffected by the whirlpool of being (*saṁsāra*); and solar, for those powers of self-awareness are present in it that secure the *auton*'s rule.

---

[19] This is a reference to the views—designated "happyendist" by Julius Evola—according to which everyone eventually attains liberation. Those who awaken not as a result of autonomous effort, but at the end of a cosmic era—when all returns into the *Metaphysicum Absolutum*—experience an awakening as regards their self-identity that is equivalent to annihilation.

296 ♦ The reason why there is only one primordial tradition is that there is only one metaphysics, and the reason why there is only one metaphysics is that there is only one Being.

297 ♦ Tradition can never be identified with mere metaphysical doctrines or with doctrinal symbology, and even less with the archaic documents presenting them. Tradition signifies the *total* acceptance of a world and the *total* refusal of another world.

298 ♦ Tradition is nothing other than "recollection" in a metaphysical sense, and the conveyance of the presence of a connection with the origin. Modernity, however, is not only the lack of this recollection, but at the same time it is the *denial* of this metaphysical recollection and is furthermore an endeavor aimed at the destruction of all representations of this recollection.

299 ♦ The most sinister thing comes into existence and lasts forever if something survives, but not truly; for this is much worse than its disappearing. This is because if something does not survive in its true form, it will sooner or later assume a function as a caricature and antithesis of the original.[20]

300 ♦ Each and every language is a tradition.

---

[20] This refers especially to those legitimate traditional, spiritual, and initiatory organizations that have survived continually, but whose original characteristics have gradually faded away or have even become their direct opposites.

301 ♦ In the earthly-human world, there cannot be a greater and tenser bipolar opposition than the opposition between Tradition and anti-tradition, or traditionality and anti-traditionality.

302 ♦ Anti-tradition can be understood only from within tradition; it cannot be understood on its own.

303 ♦ Since the offensive form of anti-traditionality appeared, even the slightest compromise between traditionality and anti-traditionality marks an enormous anti-traditional triumph.[21]

304 ♦ A traditional man should become a *scholar* of anti-traditionality.

Anti-traditional Forces

305 ♦ Anti-traditionality is nothing other than creating confusion in the relationship between the world of becoming and the center of the world of becoming, so as to make it impossible to find one's way back to the center.

---

[21] An example: "Catholic–Marxist dialogues always implied the Church going on the defensive and Marxism's success—regardless of the invariable weakness of the Marxists' performance in such dialogues in comparison with the Catholics'. This was due to the very fact that in ecclesiastic circles the discussion was not about sending Marxists to the stake, but about the possibility of finding corresponding views even among their opposing views. This marked the Church's weakness. For the Marxists, the important thing was not the dialogues' outcome, but that the Church started to 'court' them" (András László).

Anti-traditional Forces

306 ♦ Anti-traditionality is no mental question, just as it is no emotional question either; it is not a question of a mental defect, just as it is not a question of an emotional disturbance. Anti-traditionality is a question of *habitus*: the outlook of an entirely new, degenerated type of man.

307 ♦ The forces manipulating the world, so that they can work undisturbed, want to achieve two things: first of all that their very existence be questioned, but if this does not work, then at least that they appear to be invincible.

308 ♦ The dark forces operating in the world also practice riding the tiger, but it is in fact a *counter-riding the tiger*. True, they also ride the tiger, yet not by sitting on its back, but by clinging to its belly and letting themselves be carried by it.[22]

309 ♦ Disintegration is also visible on the surface. The act of disintegration, however, is always beneath the surface, and hence much more difficult to notice.

310 ♦ The path leading to chaos is not yet chaotic but is only so in its final phase. For even though a force that creates chaos does so along its way, it must necessarily become structured into the dark order of things.

---

[22] "Riding the tiger" is a Tantric symbol of Far-Eastern origin. The tiger is the symbol of great destructive forces which dissolve the world of becoming. According to the Tantric tradition, the yogi is able to "straddle" or "ride" these forces and can then turn them in the direction of realization. Hence those forces for example, sexuality or fighting—by which the common man is bound more and more by the world of becoming, may carry the yogi towards his ultimate goal.

311 ♦ If we are to define, in the most general manner, the rule that the world is presently under, then "scotasmocracy" would be the aptest term.[23]

312 ♦ The *genus* under which all of today's ruling trends belong, and of which these latter are mere adaptations to their own domain, is *scotasmocracy*, that is, the rule of darkness.

313 ♦ In the disintegration of the world, the same types of forces operate as those pertaining to the disintegration of the processes of consciousness in the narrow or strict sense of the word.

314 ♦ That which is in opposition to the plane that is above life is ultimately in opposition to life itself—for life is vitalized from the plane that is above life.

315 ♦ As the forces of modernity first annihilate the connection to the supra-natural, thus ruining man's relationship with nature, and only then destroy nature itself, in the same way they first destroy what is connected to that which transcends life, and only then annihilate life itself.

316 ♦ Arhythmicity is one of the most dangerous weapons of anti-traditionality against all aspects of life.

317 ♦ First they only disseminate the idea that he who abides by his principles is a fool (though he is not), and then the time comes that, indeed, fools alone abide by their principles...

---

[23] "Scotasmocracy" is András László's neologism; it denotes the "rule of darkness."

318 ♦ Those things that are usually designated as superstitions are in fact innocent and harmless superstitions. The adverse and harmful superstitions appear in totally different forms: as evolutionism, as anti-hierarchical concepts, as the belief in the equality of mankind, and as all those phenomena which belong to the domain of humanism in the philosophical sense.

319 ♦ Though in romantic anti-modernity a resistance against the dark forces of the modern world also appears, yet into this same resistance those claws are clutched which, out of the darkness, reach for the soul of man.

320 ♦ It is the inherent nature of every destructive force to finally undermine itself as well.

THE DARK AGE

321 ♦ The significance of modernity, wherein man falls increasingly subject to negative forces, can only be properly measured by those who know that becoming a subject even to positive forces is also a negative thing.

322 ♦ Modernity is *itself* anti-traditionality.

323 ♦ Modernity is an offensive form of anti-traditionality.

324 ♦ *Kali-yuga* means that what is beneath my personal self begins to increasingly determine my personal self, in the sense that it hinders the reduction of my personal self into my supra-personal Self.

325 ◆ Modernity is that which is hostile to realization.

326 ◆ Modern man is modern—that is, anti-traditional, anti-spiritual, and anti-metaphysical—because with his outlook and tendencies he turns not towards the Source but towards the end of the currents, a kind of ocean in a negative sense.[24]

327 ◆ Modernity is *anti-center*—but this in no way disturbs the center. Being anti-center disturbs the effort aimed at reaching the center.

328 ◆ Modernity is *conformization*—the way to conformity always going in the direction of the lowest.

329 ◆ *Kali-yuga* is mainly characterized by a passionate clinging to the continuous deterioration and disintegration of the consciousness.

330 ◆ The final phase of *kali-yuga* is the period when the poisons that have been held back are finally unleashed.

331 ◆ "Being devoured": this is the fundamental term for what the rule of darkness realizes: being devoured, which is followed by annihilation.

---

[24] The ocean is simultaneously a symbol of both the positive and negative extremes of possibilities: as a positive symbol, it symbolizes that divine totality of God's being which is the spiritual wayfarer's ultimate goal; as a negative symbol, it represents dissolution into the unqualified root-nature of the world of becoming (Sanskrit *nirguṇa mūla prakṛti*), into pure passive potentiality. Naturally, this latter is equivalent to the annihilation of individual identification, that is, of the very individual involved in the process.

332 ♦ *Kali-yuga* is not only a state but a threatening and devouring *throat*.

333 ♦ The disintegrating forces of darkness are living forces, but death-dealing living forces.

334 ♦ As a human life subjugated to illness is not only ill but is also spreading illness, so in the same way a "dark" man is not only dark but is also spreading darkness.

335 ♦ The only reason why the forces of darkness are able to take over the world is because they have already gained power in the soul.

336 ♦ What surrounds man is the reflection of his inner world.

337 ♦ It can be said with slight exaggeration that everything maintained in the present world is false: either utterly valueless, or explicitly representing some kind of dark counter-value.

338 ♦ While the present *qua* temporal interval may have some positive manifestations, it is only insofar as they do not represent the present time as modern present time.

339 ♦ What prevails at present is so bad that what is slightly better than this still cannot be considered at all good.

340 ♦ For being an *ārya*—that is, twice-born—today, one must be *thrice-born*: he must be born as an *anārya*, he must be born in a way that potential *ārya*ness somehow comes alive within him, and finally he must be born as a full member of an *ārya* caste.²⁵

341 ♦ *Kali-yuga* is present in the consciousness (in the strict sense of the word), in the human psyche, and in the spiritual manifestations and deeds of man, just as it is present in the surrounding world, in buildings, in music, in the various manifestations of artistic trends, and in the very processes of nature. Wherever man directs his attention, be it inward or outward, he is everywhere surrounded and ruled by a world which is under the aegis of anti-traditionality—that is, by being cut off from God, heaven, transcendence, superiority, and the essence.

342 ♦ The present *qua* modern age, that is, an era anti-traditional in the extreme, is the era when negatives dominate. And this is true even on the level of the most base profanities: for example, even a young and healthy man feels bad much more often than good, and he is far more depressive, sad, and gloomy than luminous, happy, and joyous.

343 ♦ The present is—as René Guénon put it—"the crisis of the modern world." Yet, the modern world without any inner crisis is *ab ovo* the crisis of the world itself. Therefore, when this same crisis itself enters a crisis, this will occur not in the sense as though a traditional world were to replace the modern world, but in the sense that the modern world

---

²⁵ In India originally, only those could become full members of the three upper—*ārya*—castes (Sanskrit *brāhmaṇa varṇa, kṣatriya varṇa, vaiśya varṇa*) who underwent a caste-initiation. These three castes' full members were designated twice-born (Sanskrit *dvija*). Those belonging to the fourth—*anārya*, that is, non-*ārya*—caste did not need to actualize their caste-membership through caste-initiation.

The Dark Age

as one built on materialism—that is, a concept representing lifelessness, destruction, and even active death-forces—reaches a phase when the destructive and necrotizing forces let loose by materialism begin to disintegrate the modern world itself.

344 ♦ Modernity is no stiffened, static reality, but a dynamic process which ceaselessly endeavors to make itself ever darker.

345 ♦ It is not a question of a simple monotonous descent. Phases of sudden halts, sharp falls, and slow sinking alternate—but these do occur during the process of a monotonous descent.

346 ♦ Exactly as even in the totally demential phase of *paralysis progressiva* there are *lucida intervalla*, but they appear more and more rarely and are less and less luminous, so too in this terminal phase of *kali-yuga* there can be *lucida intervalla*, but those who consider processes in their overall context cannot be deceived by these.

347 ♦ Modernity is just *now* maximal.

348 ♦ Once, darkening could be perceived over fifty or a hundred years. Today, it is perceivable over every five years.

349 ♦ An age in which wisdom means prudence and cleverness means sly cunning; an age where honor is associated with silliness and lunacy; and an age where—here comes the saddest part!—honesty is often connected to shallow minds and pathological mental disorders cannot be anything other than an age with a downward end.

350 ♦ An age that allows more opportunities for darkness than for light is quite justly considered damned.

351 ♦ Nothing better illustrates the nature of an era than what is successful in it: the superior or the inferior, the good or the bad, the angelic or the demonic. And today—from a "bookmaker's" point of view—the victory of the worse is incomparably more probable than that of the better.

352 ♦ Today, anyone whose aim is decline, failure, and fall can be sure of his success.

353 ♦ Everything oriented towards the fall today begins with huge advantages from the outset.

354 ♦ The truly spiritual axiom *omnia vincit veritas* holds true today, broadly speaking, only in eschatological perspectives.

355 ♦ Nowadays, darkness does not live on reservations, but flourishes everywhere, whereas spirituality does not *even* live on reservations.

356 ♦ In the past five hundred years, a new type of man has appeared who rejoices if something or someone turns out to be valueless, base, or outright non-existent. Only a degenerated type is capable of rejoicing if the world becomes poorer.

357 ♦ Most modern theories are untrue to such an extent that the views diametrically opposed to them are also false.

358 ♦ Most modern concepts are untrue to such an extent that it is not enough to replace them with concepts opposing them by 180 degrees, but they must be replaced with concepts opposing them by 540 degrees.

359 ♦ *Kali-yuga* cannot leave any discipline intact: it is massively present in each.

360 ♦ Into the overall obscuration, particular, intensifying, and darkening forces join on the planes of different processes of consciousness: distinct forces attack every process of consciousness one by one, and each of them has its own "devil."

361 ♦ Contemporary man has gradually built a denatured world for himself: he is already cut off from the supra-natural, and now he is about to break away from the natural as well.

362 ♦ The characteristic of the modern world is not so much that miracles are becoming quite few and far between, but rather that there has been a nearly absolute exhaustion of the spiritually-orientating power of miracles. If, for instance, someone appeared who surpassed all the previous magicians and wandered across the world and resurrected all the dead in the cemeteries, what would happen then? Would everyone convert, crying "peccavi"? Probably not. They would probably shrug it off by saying: "There's always something."

363 ♦ Behind today's most complicated theories there mostly lies an immeasurable poverty of thought.

364 ♦ The specific blindnesses of the dark age as a rule cloak themselves in rationalism.

365 ♦ The forces of darkness operate with some kind of subconscious consciousness and clock-like regularity so that positives can manifest only at the point when they can no longer produce any real effect.

366 ♦ Machines are demonic because they contribute to the emergence of considerable alienation between producer, production, and product—which is always accompanied by an inner alienation.

367 ♦ Though technology does not a priori contradict spirituality, in general it stands in the way of spiritual endeavors because it stems from a mentality that is based on loss of self and self-denial in a negative sense.

368 ♦ It is never possible to leave Earth in an earthly manner.

369 ♦ Wherever man goes with his earthly devices, he always takes his earthly conditions within himself.

370 ♦ The degeneration wrought by the power of money is already beyond the realm of money as a concrete means of payment.

371 ♦ There is only one form of payment more demonic than time wage, and that is piece-rate pay. While in the case of the former the mere quantity of time spent on working is taken into consideration, in the case of the latter it is the number of the products the worker produces.

372 ✦ Although journalism is incapable even of creating dark counter-ideas, the satanic forces operating behind journalism are well capable of this.

373 ✦ There might be peoples who will not partake in the new golden age, but there are no peoples who would not partake in the dark age.

374 ✦ The aim is not to reverse the process of *kali-yuga*, but on the contrary, to reach its end as quickly as possible. Nevertheless, the unconditional values must be preserved even during this process of disintegration.

375 ✦ The forces of darkness and the forces of light in some respects have the same aims in the present age: to make *kali-yuga* reach its end. But whereas the forces of darkness tend to annihilate the true values as well, the forces of light tend to maintain the true values even amidst the course of *kali-yuga* so that one day they can serve the establishment of a new golden age.

376 ✦ One has to accommodate himself to the modern world so that its powers will not wear one out—but not in the sense of bending and assimilating to it, but as a kind of acclimatization; because he who adjusts to it will not serve the age but resist it.

377 ✦ Despite all its deviation, deterioration, and dissipation, today's world and its inherent tendencies point toward one direction: the direction of *nothingness*.

378 ✦ The Being *in se* is not poisoned; *in alio*, however, it is poisoned, and lethally so.

Postmodernity

379 ♦ Postmodernity is a final and disintegrated state within modernity: that which is modern, but already disintegrated.

380 ♦ Modernity precludes all premodern institutions. Postmodernity, on the contrary, allows what it incorporates not to be formally modern—but does not tolerate anything not essentially modern. This is why the postmodern must essentially be more modern than even the most modern, otherwise it could not foster that destructive *opus* in which it will reach its purpose.

381 ♦ The postmodern state, in which everything can be manifested without any real consequence, and in which everything will be free and yet nothing will matter, must be accomplished before everything falls apart in postmodernity. Without this, the final disintegration will not come about, since certain positive remnants would always remain.

382 ♦ Precisely outlined worldviews—that is, those with sharp outlines—are extremely dangerous for the dark processes of postmodernity. When such worldviews also have a universal perspective, they are the most dangerous of all.

383 ♦ If postmodernity had an underpinning worldview, it would be post-Marxism, for within the scope of the latter it is easiest to discredit *all* worldviews.

384 ♦ Post-Marxism as a worldview is not only insignificant in itself, but what is much worse is that it makes everything else insignificant as well.

385 ♦ Let us admit, says post-Marxism, that we do not know whether being determines consciousness, or consciousness determines being. What does this mean? It means that according to this approach not only being, but—*horribile dictu!*—consciousness as well, and even their relation to one another, are *objective realities existing independently of consciousness*, of which nothing can be known about either of them with certainty.

Perspectives of the Future

386 ♦ Once it took centuries for decline to be perceivable descent; today it takes mere decades, and we are approaching the time when it will be possible to measure it in years, then in months, in weeks, and even in days. Indeed, the time may come when a sensible man wakes up in the morning to realize that during his nightly rest the world has significantly declined; and in the evening, he will go to sleep knowing that he is falling asleep in a significantly more degenerated world than the one he woke up in.

387 ♦ The *pralaya* following *kali-yuga* is neither the discharge of the withheld poisons, nor the age of becoming intoxicated as *kali-yuga* is, but it will be the age of intoxication with the emitted poisons.[26]

---

[26] Each era—including *kali-yuga*—is introduced by a pre-dissolution period (Sanskrit *pūrva-pralaya*) and followed by a post-dissolu-

388 ♦ People become aware of crises and catastrophes only when they are obvious in their extremes: cataclysmic floods, earthquakes, epidemics, famine.

389 ♦ We are not far from the moment when even the truest assertions will become petty wisdom.

390 ♦ It is not impossible that the time will come when some will accept traditionality—but from an *anti-traditional* stance. They will begin to *tinker with* Evola and Guénon—like with Heidegger nowadays: "How interesting." And then we will see the infamous miracle...

391 ♦ The effect of man's deterioration will make itself felt on deeper and deeper levels during the advancement of the dark age. At present, almost everyone is suffering from pneumatosis, and a considerable number of men suffer from psychosis as well; and it will not take long for that psychosis to become absolutely common. And there will also come a time when everyone will suffer from somatosis, particularly from somatosis developed in the intrauterine stage.[27]

392 ♦ Pneumatosis, psychosis, and somatosis develop because—to put it in the first-person singular—I come into conflict with myself.

---

tion period (Sanskrit *uttara-pralaya*). Hence, wedged in between two successive ages there is always the post-dissolution period of the first and the pre-dissolution period of the second.

[27] Pneumatosis, psychosis, and somatosis are general spiritual, psychic, and corporeal diseases, respectively, which of course manifests in specific ailments.

393 ♦ The time will come—and it is not far off—when technological civilization will collapse under its own weight.

394 ♦ The present quantitative proliferation of the human world will be followed by a likewise quantitative impoverishment and decline.

395 ♦ Which golden age, the primordial or a new one? Both. There is no real difference between the two: he restores the previous golden age, and he wishes to create the new golden age.

Spiritual Deviation—Spiritual Deceit

396 ♦ Deviationology, the study of deviations, is an inherent part of paradoseology, the knowledge of tradition.

397 ♦ It is out of the question that all non-materialistic trends should ally with one another against materialism. There are trends that appear to be spiritual but actually serve tendencies even darker than materialist atheism.

398 ♦ Those coming from India, and more recently even Tibet, to Europe and America, provide some sort of spiritual help, as it were, to Western men who have sunk into materialism. They do not actually help, however, but instead carry out a rather comprehensive, dark, and demonic mission.

399 ♦ The modern world has no initiation, and the modern world has no related spiritual path, for the modern world has extinguished the old mysteries, and new mysteries cannot arise in this world. All that can be spiritually manifested in this world can only be realized against the modern world and against its forces.

400 ✦ As authentic initiation recedes from the world, so do pseudo-initiation and counter-initiation take its place. As initiatory centers disappear, so do pseudo-initiatory and counter-initiatory centers proliferate by the thousand.

401 ✦ This age does not create new mysteries, as certain contemporary pseudo-spiritual trends proclaim; it rather produces new deviations in an inexhaustible manner.

402 ✦ In the past, superior men searched for decades to contact an initiatory center. Today, posters on kiosks offer half a dozen *gurus* simultaneously.

403 ✦ All the conditions that lead and keep one astray have been established today.

404 ✦ Just as certain insects are attracted to material light, so are the overwhelming majority of people attracted to spiritual darkness.

405 ✦ Darkness cannot be recognized by declaring itself to be dark. Things cannot be accepted at their face value. Most things are not what they say or reveal about themselves.

406 ✦ Nothing can provide *ab ovo* protection against spiritual deviation. The only way one can avoid deviation is with one's own spiritual vigilance and awareness.

407 ✦ Schools that do not build on conscious inner activities are without exception schools of darkness.

408 ♦ The spurious nature of pseudo-spiritual schools is obvious from the way they prescribe easily achievable tasks with merciless rigor.

409 ♦ It is not certain whether schools that focus on instruction, but do not teach any praxis, stand on the side of light; but it is certain that such schools as teach praxis stand on the side of false light, that is, darkness—either in the sense of imposture or "satanicity."

410 ♦ Today, those who, beyond an incidental conveying of doctrines, teach elements of praxis as well—and practically to anyone—can by no means be genuine masters: they are either impostors or pseudo-*gurus*, representing positively satanic forces. *Tertium non datur.*

411 ♦ (Pseudo-spirituality) The more diligent one is, the worse he fares.

412 ♦ Most contemporary spiritual doctrines are collections of commonplaces: sentimental bundles of banalities.

413 ♦ Initiation cannot be transmitted like chewing gum, since both its transmission and reception require almost supra-human qualifications, and if either is missing, the transmission cannot succeed. And today, as a rule, both are missing.

414 ♦ The false supposition that everybody can meditate and does not do so only because of certain reasons—such as being lazy—lurks in the background of the very frequent cases when one is over and over called upon to meditate.

415 ♦ One who says that he is practicing yoga (and the expression itself is already repellent) almost certainly has nothing to do with yoga. Yoga is the asceticism of spiritual transmutation.

416 ♦ It would be welcome if degenerate people had no ambitions. Unfortunately, however, many of them—and quite a significant part—do have ambitions; indeed, they have ambition-hypertrophy.

417 ♦ (Spiritism) Man's spiritual task is to grow into the supra-human state of being, aiming at the absolute; and not to transport different entities from other states of being into the material state.

418 ♦ Occultisms permeated by evolutionism have as a common characteristic the *happy end*: though floundering and failing again and again, each one still progresses.

419 ♦ (Reincarnationism) During incarnations, people pass through grave tribulations, are gravely jeopardized, and they are on the verge of failing, but in the end—as in a Hollywood movie—everything turns out for the best.

420 ♦ Every vital force roused inadequately—that is, not permeated by the spirit—functions as a death-force.

421 ♦ That pseudo-spiritual paths do not always end up in mental catastrophes is in fact caused by a defect: laziness.

422 ♦ It is not only that true spirituality gradually loses ground; spiritual deviations themselves are also rapidly declining—which but makes them all the more faulty and dangerous.

423 ♦ *Der Teufel ist Gottes Teufel*: "The Devil is the Devil of God."

Nature & the Supra-Natural

424 ♦ Man's origin is essentially not natural, which can also be said about nature itself.

425 ♦ The protection of the superhuman, that which is above life, and the supernatural should always precede the protection of man, life, and nature.

426 ♦ Today, surpassing the naïve view of nature takes place by means of abstraction—whereas the naïve concept should in fact be surpassed by a process of surpassing: towards transcending the naïve view. Abstraction is always twofold: it is abstraction from the concrete reality of naïvely-grasped entities of a particular reality—but at the same time, it is also abstraction from the spirit. By contrast, transcending is real surpassing, since it surpasses the naïve view of nature towards the origin of being.

427 ♦ Everything that is against the supernatural also turns, sooner or later, against the natural.

Humanism

428 ♦ Humanism is a typically anti-human view which strives to despoil man of his own supra-human origin and of his awareness concerning his own supra-human goals.

429 ♦ Humanism is a peculiar way and concept for the preparation of sub-humanness.

430 ♦ Humanism is not simply humanism, but it is the *Homo humus'* humanism, that of the man turning towards and bound to the Earth.

431 ♦ From the philosophical point of view, humanism does not mean the achievement of humanitarian goals, but that man wants to define his destiny merely on the human level, and with tools of the merely human order.

MATERIALISM

432 ♦ Basically, there are two kinds of materialism: material materialism and formal materialism. The latter is equivalent to declared materialism, while the former is a consequence of the consciousness' impotence: when the spirit's power is unable to resist the influence of psychic and corporeal contingencies coming from underneath. The latter's subsidiary worldview might be anything, including even extreme idealism.

433 ♦ Materialism is the philosophical school that stylizes and articulates naïve realism—that is, the view that is inclined to see only the surface of surfaces.

434 ♦ Materialistic objectivism is the most inferior philosophical approach.

435 ♦ Materialism separates man from the superior worlds not only by its teachings, and not even mainly through its teachings, but primarily through the situations and living conditions it establishes, since what becomes corrupt also depraves, and what is destroyed also works as a destructive force through its vestigial nature.

436 ♦ There was no materialism prior to the sixth century before Christ, and it would have been impossible.

437 ♦ The English Civil War had a Protestant nature. The "great" French Revolution was deist. The Russian Revolution was outright atheistic. Protestantism → deism → atheism: these are the grades of the descent of modern times.

438 ♦ The real materialist-atheist is actually a disguised anti-theist: he knows that God exists, but he will still deny it out of revenge. He is angry with God because He forbids him something, and since he cannot bear to be restricted, he denies His existence.[28]

439 ♦ Man generally considers something real when he is unable to cope with it, and the more powerless he is, the more real he considers that thing to be. This is why the sense of touch is the chief faculty of verification, since this is when one meets with the most impenetrable, against which man is the most helpless—when in fact what one experiences is only the weight of his own body or of a part of his body. At the same time, there is nothing less real for the man of the dark age than that which is so much in his power that it is identical with him—to wit, himself. He is unable to apprehend himself as the subject of every action because he

---

[28] According to one of the slogans of the Paris Commune: "There is no God, but even if there were, He should be shot."

does not experience any resistance against and impotence towards his very self. This is called *viparyaya* in the Hindu tradition.

440 ♦ No matter how much the Marxist view made itself hated during the socialist era, its marked impact is clearly visible even on those who opposed it.

441 ♦ An anti-religious counter-religion elevated to the dignity of a state religion: such was materialist atheism in the countries of Bolshevist terror.

OBJECTIVISM

442 ♦ Naïve realism is a very common worldview with which nobody identifies, since nobody declares that "I am a naïve realist."

443 ♦ (Naïve realism) The error is never in the perception itself, but in the relationship between perception and thinking.

444 ♦ Each objectivism is the result of some kind of defect in self-awareness.

POLITICS

445 ♦ Politics only motivated by politics can only be negative; only metapolitically-inspired politics is justified. And likewise, apolitically-motivated apoliticism cannot be but negative as well, for only the metapolitically-inspired apoliticism is justified.

446 ✦ We do not need to go too far back in time to reach a state where there was no sign of Leftism whatsoever.

447 ✦ As the governmental, political, and social projection of traditionality is Rightism, even so is the governmental, political, and social projection of anti-traditionality Leftism.

448 ✦ When traditionality manifests in the earthly-human-social-governmental sphere, then it manifests as Rightism—and not as moderate Rightism, but as maximal rightism.

449 ✦ The spirit is *ab ovo* aristocratic.

450 ✦ The spirit is always theocratic, autocratic, and aristocratic.

451 ✦ In Rightism there is no such thing as moderation.

452 ✦ The criterion of each genuine domination is spiritual superiority, the *suprematia realivera*: the actual and true supremacy. If the actual and true supremacy is not present, then the *dominatio*, the domination, cannot be a real domination. And if the domination is not real, then one cannot speak of *potestas*, of the real possession of power, but only of the illegitimate usurpation of power (*usurpatio illegitima potestatis*). Unreal *dominatio* is sufficient for the latter. Why is it not real? Because there is no actual and true supremacy, since one cannot simply be "nominated" for supremacy.

Usurpers of power can be appointed to the appropriate posts; the representatives of actual supremacy, however, cannot be appointed, because they either possess supremacy or they do not. If there is no actual *dominatio*, then the usurpation of power appears, and even therein the usurpation only of certain elements of power that are related to aggression. The usurper can only usurp the aggressive features of power, because anything else would necessitate actual *strength*. Aggression does not require the actual power of a personality; it only needs machine-guns and batons.

453 ♦ Mundane *suprematia* (supremacy) is based on spiritual *suprematia*, mundane *dominatio* (domination) on spiritual *dominatio*, and mundane *potestas* (power) on spiritual *potestas*. This was the principle of the ancient monarchies.

454 ♦ The further the dark age unfolds, the more the Center-consciousness disappears, as does the Center's political projection: the idea of the kingdom.

455 ♦ The monarch is—in his essence—motionless: he is like the center or the axis.

456 ♦ *Iupiter Stator* means not only "Jupiter the Founder," but also "Jupiter the Stayer." This is because establishing something is the same as halting something.

457 ♦ The divine king of Rome, *Iupiter Stator*, was at once Founder and Stayer, who by virtue of his *stator*-nature maintained atemporal eternity in the temporal world. The original meaning of the State is of an altogether divine nature: it is no apparatus, no aggregate of offices, but the representation of the unmoved divine presence in the *saṁsār*ian world.

458 ♦ The non-monarchic state is in fact no state, no *status*—because the State in its original sense is not an apparatus but a living organism.

459 ♦ As the body is greater than a cell but can be divided into cells, even so is sacred society greater than the individual but can be divided into individuals. The value of the whole is always greater than the sum of its parts.

460 ♦ The State—in the original sense of the word—is not at all an "enforcement organization." This is so not only because force is the most inferior manifestation of power, but also because the State is not merely an organization, but a living organism.

461 ♦ "The land belongs to those who cultivate it." But not only to them: it belongs more to rent it in order to cultivate it. And it belongs most of all to those who rent it out for cultivation. Above all, it belongs to God. This is the hierarchy of feudal proprietorship.

462 ♦ The anti-Right-wing attitude is at the same time always anti-traditional, even if those who hold this view are not fully conscious of it—merely because the very fact that they are not fully aware of what they represent is itself anti-traditional.

463 ♦ The pure forms of *feudum* and *imperium* can be disagreeable only for those whose mental-spiritual life lacks even the prefiguration of hierarchical differentiation.

464 ♦ Large-scale wars are engendered mainly to achieve the situation that follows in their wake. In Europe prior to

the First World War, traditionality had been more or less preserved by four empires: the German Empire, the Austro-Hungarian Monarchy, the Russian Tsarist Empire, and the Turkish Sultanate. All four disappeared partly during the war and partly after it, regardless of the side they fought on. The abolition of these four empires would have been impossible without this war. And the Second World War was engendered in part in order to ruin both the Eastern part of Europe by the Soviet and the Western part of Europe by American influence—in different ways, but essentially to the same effect, so that at a given moment these two interpenetrate each other and direct these two aspects of taintedness towards and within each other.

465 ✦ A government led by spirituality does not tolerate parliamentary comedies.

466 ✦ (Constitutional monarchy) As the consciousness focusing on itself cannot be subject to bodily contingencies, thus is the sovereign never dependent on those over whom he reigns.

467 ✦ The nadir of the present world situation is epitomized by the fact that nothing can oppose the infernal Bolshevist terror other than an inferior, spiritless institution that is not regulated by superior powers such as democracy.

468 ✦ Democracy as a radically anti-traditional and anti-spiritual institution has as its actual antithesis not the equally anti-traditional and anti-spiritual terrorist dictatorship, but the reign of the spirit.

469 ♦ Despite the superficial differences between liberalism and Communism, their essential identity reveals itself in their most extreme common *permaximum*[29]: in anarchism. This means that both of them principally derive from anarchism.

470 ♦ Anarchism is Leftism at its purest.

471 ♦ When people imagine Communism as some sort of ideal society, their imagination usually only extends as far as the first day, when they go shopping and take home as much as they want. How the shelves will get refilled the next day, and who will produce those products, is beyond their vision.

472 ♦ The tenets of Communism are inferior, distorted, and in addition—fortunately—unrealizable.

473 ♦ In the nineteenth century, nationalism and internationalism were two parallel anti-traditional and anti-spiritual trends of Leftism. The classical example was the extreme Leftist Sándor Petőfi, who was both a nationalist to a chauvinistic extreme and a rabid internationalist at the same time.[30]

474 ♦ Each and every view that seizes upon a biological form of association not on the level of the kind of essences

---

[29] *"Permaximum"* is András László's Latin-based neologism referring to a thing's most extreme, ultimate way of realization.
[30] Sándor Petőfi (1823–49) is said to have been one of the greatest Hungarian poets and was one of the leaders of the 1848 Revolution in Hungary. His name has been given to streets even in the most obscure Hungarian villages. (Translator's note)

a particular biological substrate may carry, but on the level of blood ties, is a manifestation of disintegrated thought.[31]

475 ✦ If a collective category is only the aggregate of its participants, then it always remains inferior to the level of its most basic elements.

476 ✦ (The House of Árpád) The members of the Turul dynasty were not Hungarians, but Turuls. Being a Turul was superior to being Hungarian—and this is why they could become the kings of the Hungarians.

477 ✦ The reason for the close connection between the Right-wing attitude and nationalism is not that the essence of the Right-wing attitude is nationalism, but because the Left has heavily shifted in the direction of internationalism.

478 ✦ After having exhausted nationalism's destructive possibilities, the subversive forces working in the world today came to believe that the time was ripe for switching to internationalism.

479 ✦ Inorganic totalitarianism, which has an anagogic beginning and a katagogic end, persecutes everything that is not in accordance with its ideology. Democratism opens the door to every kind of rubbish.[32]

---

[31] Typical examples of this are the ethnic and popular forms of nationalism.

[32] Inorganic totalitarianism has anagogic intentions, that is, surging up from underneath, but always a katagogic outcome, that is, pulling into the abyss from above. Its antithesis is organic totalitarianism, which has katagogic intentions, that is, acting downwards from above, but always has an anagogic outcome, that is, lifting

480 ♦ Metaphysical tradition knows two kinds of peace: *pax post victoriam lucis*—that is, peace after the victory of Light, and *pax post victoriam tenebratum*—peace after the victory of Darkness.

481 ♦ What we need is the dictatorship of light. The dictatorship of the spirit...

EGALITARIANISM—DEMOCRACY—LIBERALISM

482 ♦ Egalitarianism always means levelling downward. Every equalization is based on lowering.

483 ♦ Complete legal equality can only be achieved only as an equality resulting from the complete lack of all rights.

484 ♦ The view that "all men are equal" is in fact not the result of a logical deduction, but the manifestation of a disposition. Egalitarianism is based not on a recognition, but on an inclination. He who equalizes undervalues himself to start with—only to continue the denial of his own dignity through the general denial of dignity. For he who is unable to discover dignity within himself will not be able to see it in others, either.

485 ♦ Even the most dull-brained and the most confused followers of the idea of equality know very well that there are differences among men, both in the horizontal and vertical sense of their relations, but they pretend this is not the case.

---

upwards from below—and this is nothing other than monarchism.

486 ♦ False rhetoric: "All men are equal." Even the most extreme egalitarian democrat does not believe in it. True, he might sacrifice his very life for it, but he would still not believe in it—because even he himself organizes his life according to the exact opposite principle.

487 ♦ Liberalism supposes the legal equality of those men who in fact all want the same thing: the abolishment of the predominance of quality.

488 ♦ Liberalism not only represents the view that all men are equal, but it also does its best to abolish quality in order to make all men indeed equal.

489 ♦ The principle of equality applies only to those who accept this principle. Should anyone try to question egalitarianism, he will find himself thrown out of the circle of people who possess equal rights before the law.

490 ♦ The incoherence of liberalism is shown inter alia by the fact that if one tried to consistently apply its main principles, one would need to welcome anti-liberalism as well.

491 ♦ The genuine liberal should not be more enthusiastic about anything other than that which differs from his own views; and the more different it is, the more enthusiastic about it he should be.[33]

---

[33] That is—*ad absurdum*—a consistent liberal should be the most enthusiastic about radically anti-liberal ultra-Rightism—since it is so ravishingly "different."

492 ♦ As the genuine liberal should set a high value on anti-liberals, so should the genuine anarchist be enthusiastic about the opponents of anarchism—as thinkers of an alternative way.

493 ♦ Either stupid or malicious. *Tertium non datur*.[34]

494 ♦ Liberalism is firstly against *libertas*, secondly against liberality, and finally against liberalism, since an approach that sets out to make all views relative and also undermine all other views inevitably turns against itself.

495 ♦ From a certain point of view, everybody is "one who thinks differently."

496 ♦ The committed adherents of alternative thought do not adhere to all alternative thought, but only a certain kind of alternative thought.

497 ♦ It appears that the criticism of the freedom of opinion does not fall within the domain of freedom of opinion.

498 ♦ As much as the battle of liberalism against terrorism is futile, so is its fight against every kind of superiority effective.

499 ♦ The different forms of democracy—liberal and dictatorial—are unacceptable primarily not on a political, but a spiritual basis. This is so because if the spirit were to man-

---

[34] This alternative often appears not only in political, but also in spiritual—pseudo-spiritual—relations.

ifest in the domain of politics, it would not manifest as democracy.

500 ♦ Democracy means that the periphery rather than the center rules: not the axis-like, motionless mover and stayer—that is, the king—but that which is peripherally moved and halted: the people.

501 ♦ If one thinks that everybody could be involved in the administration of the world's affairs, what one declares thereby is that in connection with the individual man or—to put it in first person singular—in connection with myself, it is without any importance what dark unconscious forces affect and drive me, and their presence and effect is of the same value as the presence and effect of the forces of spiritual light.

502 ♦ Forces of the *démos*, whether they manifest in one's consciousness or in the world, are not ascendent forces, but surge up from underneath, deconstructing the upper according to the lower and finally dragging everything downwards.

503 ♦ If one embraces the tenet of "majority rules," to be consistent one should also accept the domination of the dark, dim, and confused mental vortices within himself.

504 ♦ "Majority rules!"—This can be heard among little children when they are arguing about whether they should play tag or hide-and-seek. And this can be the only domain where democracy might be justified.

505 ♦ That the people are completely ineligible to vote is demonstrated *inter alia* by the fact that when the people do not elect what certain political powers prefer (and after each election there are always such political powers, viz. those who lost the election), then the people are said to have been misled. Then, when the people elect what these powers approve of, then the same say that the people have taken a wise decision. After all, what sort of legitimacy does someone have who can be misled?

506 ♦ (Democracy) The public can be made to accept anything with proper preparation.

507 ♦ "Popular sovereignty"—nobody believes in this, since it is impossible to believe that a public which can be manipulated without any restraint has any kind of superiority.

508 ♦ Undoubtedly everyone is competent to decide what would please him at the present moment: when they are hungry, thirsty, or sleepy; what and how much they want to eat, drink, sleep; whether they feel cold or warm. But only men with high spiritual qualifications can adequately decide what they need in the long run.

509 ♦ A world where people despise their leaders is degenerate in itself. True, they despise them because they deserve disdain—but a situation such as this is subnormal in every respect: despised people take high positions, even though those who despise them enabled them to occupy those positions in the first place. This is a real vicious circle. In this way, approximately two-thirds of the people hate and despise approximately two-thirds of their own leaders, indisputably because the latter deserve it—but the story is not finished there, since inferiority penetrates everything, both those who are despised and those who despise them.

510 ♦ The term "democrat" that is adopted in the name of almost every political party today could be changed to "scotasmocrat" without much ado: Hungarian Scotasmocratic Forum, Alliance of Free Scotasmocrats, Alliance of Young Scotasmocrats, even the Christian-Scotasmocratic People's Party.[35]

511 ♦ Created beings do not elect God from among themselves.

512 ♦ Democracy, that is, the idea that the majority should rule, is nothing other than a slap in the face of the spirit.

From Supra-historicity to Sub-historicity

513 ♦ Each era, and hence also the dark age, is primarily a state of consciousness, and only secondarily a historical era.

514 ♦ While the powers of darkness and light are equally present in a great cycle (Sanskrit *mahāyuga*), but they do not manifest to an equal extent: the darkness scarcely manifests at the cycle's beginning, whereas at the cycle's end, the luminous forces manifest only faintly.

---

[35] Scotasmocracy is the "rule of darkness." The parties parodied were the parliamentarian parties of the 1990–94 election cycle: the Hungarian Democratic Forum, Alliance of Free Democrats, Alliance of Young Democrats, and the Christian-Democratic People's Party.

515 ♦ He who is confined within the cycle by the cycle's forces can transcend the cycle in two ways: either in the direction of the center, or by gradually drifting outwards from the cycle followed by a total breakaway from it. He who integrates himself into the cycle's center becomes its ruler, and the cycle's laws no longer apply to him. He who by contrast drifts out of the cycle is heading towards annihilation.

516 ♦ The adherent of the doctrine of cycles is no "cyclicist"—that is, he does not adhere to the cycles. The doctrine of cycles is not "cyclicism."

517 ♦ The essence of *kali-yuga* is that after losing his transcendent history, man lost his celestial history and his mythical history as well, and then he entered the sphere of earthly history: the sphere wherein things are happening to him, and he has lost his autonomy for shaping his own destiny. In this state, his being has become entangled in the net of relations and circumstances, and all that stood beneath him now begins to rule over him.

518 ♦ Supra-historicity was the experience of a differentiated and integrated unity; historicity is the experience of a partially differentiated but disintegrating unity; sub-historicity is that of a faintly differentiable disintegratedness—and at the same time the experience of coagulation into a mass.

519 ♦ Man's historicity is a breakaway from those forces and relations that bind him to the center of the Being (where one is aware of the essence of the Being).

520 ♦ Sub-historicity is related to the loss of autonomy to such a degree that man's individual state is transferred to a subindividual and mass-like state.

521 ♦ "Historicity": this means that things *happen* to man; that is, he does not realize his own history himself, but history simply *takes place*.

522 ♦ The way history is interpreted in the whole world today should be almost completely reversed. From the traditional point of view, the Middle Ages was not dark, but positively luminous; the Renaissance was not a rebirth, but the beginning of an agony and disintegration; and the age of Enlightenment could be justly called the age of Darkening.

523 ♦ There are historical situations wherein the postulation of God's existence is more detrimental than its denial. Such was the so-called "great" French Revolution, which introduced the "state" cult of the Supreme Being for political-tactical reasons.

524 ♦ Myth is not only truer, but also more real, than history.

525 ♦ Antiquity is the imprint of the archaic in time.

CULTURE

526 ♦

Traditionalitas Metaphysica Vera
↓
Religio Vera

This is the relationship that modernity attacks from all sides, because on one hand, it attacks each and every member of this relationship, but on the other, it attacks even more strongly the relationships themselves.[36]

527 ♦ A civilization that is not based upon culture is a pseudo-civilization; a culture that is not based upon confession is a pseudo-culture; a confession that is not based upon religion is a pseudo-confession; a religion that is not based upon tradition is a pseudo-religion.

528 ♦ Modern culture is the culture of anti-spirituality and anti-traditionality. Consequently, it can only be considered as pseudo-culture, or rather counter-culture. This term denotes counter-cultivation, that is the cultivation of man and the world in such a way and to such a degree that they are continually becoming more susceptible to the darkness instead of the light.

---

[36] That is: True metaphysical traditionality → True religion → True confession → True culture → True civilization. While the *religio* (cf. Latin *re-ligare* = "to bind," "to rebind") is the inner facet of religion turning towards the metaphysical, the *confessio* is the outer facet of religion turning towards the culture.

529 ✦ Counter-culture is no mere weakness in culture, and it does not mean that man's world is inundated with cheap things instead of higher values. The real meaning of counter-culture is that man and his world turn in a completely different direction from the one they ought to, because counter-culture cultivates the counter-rule and counter-cultivation of darkness as opposed to the rule and cultivation of light.

530 ✦ The essence of the Renaissance was not the revival of antiquity, but rather the annihilation of the traditionality held within Western Christianity. It is of course the case that a revival of certain forms of antiquity did formally take place, but substantially the very essence of Christianity—those traditional elements which originated from Greco-Roman antiquity itself—was destroyed.

531 ✦ That which is called the Enlightenment today is certainly an unambiguous darkening, and it was exactly that which was dark in it that resulted in it being called "Enlightenment": the denial of the spirit.

532 ✦ The "Enlightenment" did not simply mean that people, having left their theocentric view behind, turned their minds towards the Earth once and for all; they also set this very act—by calling it "Enlightenment"—on a pedestal.

533 ✦ Turning towards the Earth powerfully reveals decline and decay; but how degenerate this (materialistic) view has become can really be shown by the fact that this turning towards the Earth is characterized according to its opposite: not as "Endarkening," but "Enlightenment."³⁷

534 ♦ What is inferior cannot possibly delight anyone, as the inferior can never be beautiful. If one is drawn towards the inferior, it does not mean that it delights him, but rather that this is simply what corresponds to his character.

535 ♦ Modern popular music fails to fulfil the original aims of real music, which is that instead of invoking superior powers, it activates the lowest and darkest forces of the world.

536 ♦ The essence of the rock, hard, and metal variations of modern popular music is that they deliver subtle *beats* towards the deeper layers of the somatic organism in order to awaken the demoniac world bound within the somaticum.³⁸

537 ♦ The chthonic—that is, something which has a connection with subterranean forces—demonism and phantom world penetrates into man through various ecstatic states, and is in a deep and close connection with that music of Negroid origin with which the world inundates itself today.

---

[37] Manifestations of these kinds of processes in Plato's time were similarly criticized by him when he said that this attitude originated in "a very grievous sort of ignorance which is imagined to be the greatest wisdom" (*Laws* 886b).
[38] The effects of the types of music in question are not at all subtle, of course.

538 ♦ The bulk of negative processes and tendencies, be they Communism, environmental pollution, or economic crises, might be suppressed and reversed. There is, however, one process that is insuppressible, and there is not even any wish to hold it back: the rapidly increasing "not-anything-like-ness" and "featureless-ness-ification."

539 ♦ The collapse of culture will be signified neither by people losing their interest in everything, nor by the fact that cultural filth will inundate the world, but by the fact that even the most positive works will lose their values: the most succinct truths will be held to be invalid bombasts, and everything will become commonplace—even that which is not so. And the portents of this are clearly discernible already...

ART & BEAUTY

540 ♦ The sacred tendency present in the arts originally aimed at opening up a path in the world of manifestation back towards the primordial origin.

541 ♦ The true *artifex* is at the same time *pontifex*—a priest, that is, a bridge-builder: he fashions himself as a bridge and traverses himself from one end to the other, to connect transcendence with immanence within himself.

542 ♦ That which is beautiful is similar to its own essence: to its own *Ding an sich* nature.

543 ♦ It seems that today's man is ashamed of uttering the word "beautiful." Be it a poem, a musical composition, a painting, or a sculpture, a work of art is almost never considered "beautiful," but always only "pretty." Not even a woman has the right to be called beautiful, but only "pretty" or "good." In this case "good" obviously does not refer to her behavior, but rather to her sex appeal, which clearly shows that even "good" has already lost its meaning. And yet even about God it was once said: *Pulchritudo Dei infinita est*—"The beauty of God is infinite."

544 ✦ He who wants to be "richer" in infernal artistic experiences does not need to search for a long time.

545 ✦ In some sense, every picture is a self-portrait.

SCIENCE

546 ✦ The modern scientific worldview *qua* worldview is fundamentally a heresy—not only from the perspective of Catholicism, but from that of all possible religions.

547 ✦ Mechanical and dialectic materialism did not need to specifically penetrate the modern scientific worldview, for the latter arose in such a way that the different variations of materialism could immediately adopt and present it in a ready form.

548 ✦ Every physical and chemical poison is the material representation of a spiritual poison.

549 ✦ The gaseous state is superior to the liquid state, and the liquid state is in general also superior to the solid state—with one exception: for if the solid state is not amorphous but of a crystalline structure, then it is not inferior but superior to the liquid state.

550 ♦ It is of no avail for a psychologist to be proficient in psychology if he is incompetent in the psyche.

RELIGION

551 ♦ Those who know all about, say, Buddhism, but nothing about the Being and consciousness, actually do not understand Buddhism, either.

552 ♦ Religion implies such an endeavor as aims at shattering the framework immanent in the earthly sense.

553 ♦ Religion has emerged in *kali-yuga*—not, however, as a product of the darkening process, but rather as the reaction to it. Since prior to *kali-yuga* man had lived in such a near-spiritual state, that was as yet no need for specific religions or rites.

554 ♦ There are religious institutions that, having lost their purpose, necessarily wither and vanish; as in for example shamanism. However, there are also religious institutions that, having lost their essential doctrines, are still able to exist, such as and most especially Christianity, for instance.

555 ♦ Christianity can more or less function with titular bishops, contrary to shamanism, which is not likely to operate with titular shamans.

556 ♦ Totemism does not mean that a given people traces themselves back to a concrete animal ancestor, but rather that the human generation in question has been created by a will which is analogous to the will that has created the divine/demoniac spirit of a kind of animal species.

557 ♦ Religions today no longer represent metaphysical tradition. What is more, the time has arrived when we can safely declare: religions today do not represent and convey even religion any longer, but mere ragged relics of customs and shreds of lifeless doctrines. They have become as if they themselves strived for their own lowering and annihilation—and in fact they do.

558 ♦ If there were a certain being who could fulfil every sincere desire, that is a being who could behave in the way a significant number of religious people would like to see God, then this being would be merely a *saṁsāra*ic being with a wide range of power, but with a relatively inferior consciousness.

559 ♦ Prayer can always reach only that height at which it has been uttered. And since a worshipper cannot pray, even in quite exceptional moments, from a position higher than his own guardian angel's, his prayer does not go beyond his guardian angel, either. Only that request can reach God which I send out from a divine position.

560 ♦ The condition for a prayer's fulfillment is not the sincerity of our desire, but the unshakeable certainty that it will be fulfilled.

561 ♦ Faith, after all, is always faith in myself.

562 ✦ "Dialogue with God"—"God can be addressed and He can address me, too": this is but mawkishness wrapped in theological language.

563 ✦ Grace is transmission and reception of a power, wherein the receiver and beneficiary experiences his own position as a receiver and beneficiary, but does not experience the level of the grace's benefactor. Only after an inner restoration and integration does it transpire that grace can be given only by myself, and accepted only by myself.

564 ✦ Logos is the primordial unity of the powers of consciousness.

565 ✦ Theology is not necessarily religious, and religion is not necessarily theological.

566 ✦ Satan also believes that God exists; indeed, he knows it—and even so he is no believer but an atheist.

567 ✦ The depreciation of any religion entails the undermining of all religions—*including one's own religion.*

568 ✦ Those who strive for metaphysical and supra-life self-realization must leave the sphere of religion behind and attach themselves to the supra-religious state of forms, and reach for the state of the Being beyond forms. In today's dark age, forms that are still related to religion can easily lead the person who embraces them onto a path that is completely opposed to the original goals and aims of religion.

CHRISTIANITY

569 ♦ One of the main characteristics of the modern theological attitude is its covert or overt anti-ecclesiasticism.

570 ♦ Today, it is less and less possible to speak about a confrontation between the Church and the modern world—but more and more about adaptation in the sense of an assimilation that reaches even the essence. The Church is no longer an opponent, but *a part* of the modern world.

571 ♦ The gradual loss of Tradition in the Church has unfortunately reached the point where she not only openly stands against metaphysical traditionality, provided she is familiar with it at all; but she also opposes her own tradition—albeit not explicitly.

572 ♦ Christianity *ab ovo* included all the heresies, because if it had not been so, they could not have arisen. Christian Satan-worship is positively *Christian* in the sense that such an antithetical Christian religion operates in Christian terms. If the worship of Māra had developed in Buddhism, that would have been a completely different Satan-worship from Christian Satanism: a specifically Buddhist Satanism.[39]

573 ♦ "To repent of one's sin is much more important than not to sin"—although this tenet has never been explicitly formulated in Christianity's main doctrines, it has always been covertly present in Christianity.[40]

---

[39] Māra is the Satan of Buddhism.
[40] Certain Russian sects have even explicitly taught that repenting sin is more important than not to commit it.

574 ♦ The reason that the early missionaries in America could not boast about great achievements lay in the fact that, although the Native Americans considered almost all Christian teachings to be quite appealing, they could not come to terms with the idea of their being sinners. And there was certainly an attitude in Christianity according to which the less one found oneself to be sinful, the more sinful one was.

575 ♦ If we would really like to put our finger on the matter, then the Reformation should rather be called "Deformation" instead.

576 ♦ Christianity which has incorporated Tradition is reconcilable with Tradition, but Christianity without this incorporation is not.

PHILOSOPHY

577 ♦ Philosophy is no path, only an introductory course: the introductory course to the *philosophia perennis*.

578 ♦ Today it is not he who is occupied with philosophy who counts as a significant philosopher, but he who deals with a certain philosopher; he is regarded as more important if he specializes not only in a particular philosopher, but in all those who have ever dealt with him. And if someone is employed producing literature about the literature dealing with some philosopher, then he certainly studies philosophy at an exceptionally high scientific level.

579 ♦ Every philosopher, if he is *only* a philosopher, sins, primarily against himself. As soon as he begins to expound his thoughts, he immediately commits the same sin against others as well.

580 ♦ Although the armature of rationalism is rational in character, its intention to create and sustain rationalism derives from subrational tendencies.

ETHICS

581 ♦ The two poles of duality are never completely equivalent. It cannot be said that darkness, as one half of unity, is worth as much as the other half, the light, because unity can only be realized from the light-side of duality. From the darkness, unity cannot be restored. The unity of darkness and light can only be restored from the light.

582 ♦ There is no need for moral rules for that person who possesses a kind of inner light, and for whom responsibility is based upon the principle coinciding with the totality of the Being, since something either serves as a means for absolution, and then it has to be done; or impedes absolution, in which case it has to be avoided. These morals are undoubtedly pragmatic; however, they are morals oriented toward self-realization.

583 ♦ For a superior type of man, a moral commandment is only a sign, a warning. The more inferior the man in question, the more imperatively and compellingly the commandment should be asserted, event to the extent of physical coercion as a last resort. For a superior man, there are no prohibitions or demands, only signs.

584 ✦ For an inferior type of man, every moral rule is a commandment, and the more inferior the man, the more severe the commandment must be.

585 ✦ The higher hierarchical levels are that are injured, the more far-reaching the consequences will be. Therefore, from the traditional point of view, doing harm to a child is not as grave as harming a human being at the zenith of his life.

586 ✦ Sin is a consequence.

587 ✦ What is strictly prohibited for some people might even be compulsory for others in certain circumstances.

Symbology

588 ✦ If something is "merely symbolic," then it is not even symbolic anymore.[41]

589 ✦ An image *qua* image cannot be true, because in this sense it is simply one manifestation among many. It undoubtedly exists, but it does not convey any truth in itself. At the same time, every image is also a sign, because it indicates the existence of a higher reality, and in this sense it does convey truth.

---

[41] All beings are symbols of higher, principal realities; however, no being can be a pure symbol, because then it would not have its own existence distinct from the symbolized entity. If something were "merely symbolic," it could not even exist.

590 ♦ In a sense, every man is a symbol of high significance to every man, and the more intimate the acquaintance between two people, the more they are symbols to one another.

591 ♦ The revolution of the Earth is symbolic of *saṁsāra*ic existence.

592 ♦ The Buddha in human form is part of *saṁsāra*, but as a part of *saṁsāra* it symbolizes *nirvāṇa*.

EVOLUTION & INVOLUTION—PROGRESS & DECLINE

593 ♦ Metaphysical traditionality rejects the theory of evolution not because it disapproves of it, but because it does not experience it.

594 ♦ Evolutionary theories are dangerous superstitions not only because they derive the superior from the inferior, but also because they treat progress as a necessary or inevitable fact.[42]

595 ♦ Each and every animal species is a dead end along the cosmic path of the cosmic Man of hypercosmic origin—a dead end that the Universal Man rejects, but which at the same time he also calls into being, projecting it as his own mental, imaginative, and volitional product, and which he then finally steers onto the path of gradual materialization.

---

[42] In this connection, cf. the 746th aphorism.

596 ♦ "Every animal is an obsession" (Heinrich Steffens). It is not the obsession of present-day man. It is the obsession of man.

597 ♦ Animal species are projections and materializations of human forms of consciousness.

598 ♦ Theories of descent not only declare that man originates from the animals, but also that man *is* an animal.[43]

599 ♦ The relationship between languages is a death blow for all types of evolutionism: because archaic languages were far superior to and much more complex than those that came later.

600 ♦ It is trivially evident that an era's superiority is determined not by its technological standard, but by its degree of—putting it exoterically—closeness to God, or—from an esoteric point of view—closeness to Myself.

601 ♦ We could only speak about progress if we could speak about man's gradual transformation into a superior type of man. However, we can attribute several of modern man's qualities—but not superiority.

602 ♦ No doubt, the twentieth century has achieved much more in terms of technology than the last ten thousand

---

[43] This is greatly exemplified by the titles of two books by the noted evolutionist, Desmond Morris: *The Naked Ape* and *The Human Animal*. As far as we are concerned, we reject these two "flattering" titles; nevertheless, we have no objection to them when referring to Desmond Morris.

years—but nonetheless this is also true with respect to its separation from the spirit.

603 ✦ Eclipse → Separation → Fracture → Disintegration: these are the grades of the world's descent.

Woman—Matrimony—Family

604 ✦ We must be able to perceive the woman in Sophia as well as Sophia in the woman.[44]

605 ✦ A woman can achieve *nigredo* if she receives instructions from a man; a woman can achieve *albedo* if she progresses together with a man; and a woman can achieve *rubedo* if she is united with a man.[45]

607 ✦ If marriages are indeed "contracted in Heaven"—as the Christian and especially Catholic tradition teaches—then how can matrimony be interpreted so materialistically and only in its earthly aspects such that, upon the death of one party, the widowed party is considered liberated from the matrimonial bonds and is allowed to freely remarry?

608 ✦ Polygamy is perfect in the case when the number of wives is a prime number minus one—in which case, although it is not truly a prime number, the number one must

---

[44] Sophia is the eternal and most superior archetype of woman and womanhood.
[45] *Nigredo* (blackening and blackness), *albedo* (whitening and whiteness), and *rubedo* (reddening and redness) are the three ascending hierarchical grades of alchemy.

also be listed among the prime numbers. Hence, the number of wives can only be zero, one, two, four—but not three![46]

609 ♦ Even in this century there have been efforts to legalize polygamy, but—*diabolically*—the number of wives is limited to three.

610 ♦ While parents do have far-reaching responsibilities for their children, this does not mean that they should live entirely for their sake. Everyone has to do their duty, first of all strictly towards *themselves*.

THE SACRED & PROFANE ASPECT OF SEXUALITY

611 ♦ In the number two, that is, the number standing for the manifested world immersed in creation, there appears the refusal of unity, but also the affirmation of the restoration of unity.

---

[46] The reason why the number of wives is ideally "a prime number minus one" is that in this way the number of wives is completed by the number of the husband—which is always one—, that is, the number of the participants in the marital relationship will always be a prime number. Prime numbers—including the number one—are numbers that are divisible only by one or themselves, and hence every prime number constitutes an ideal, hard-to-disintegrate and hard-to-be-disintegrated, stable, closed, and perfected whole that is characterized on one hand by harmony, and on the other by autonomy (this pertains to the aggregate 0+1 as well, where zero stands for the number of wives, and one for the number of the "husband"). Though to a smaller extent, odd numbers bear similar qualities, while even numbers—except for the number two—albeit closed, are imperfect.

612 ♦ The phenomenon of sex and sexuality is not primarily psychological, but much more essential and superior: an *ontological* reality.

613 ♦ Bipolar tensions possess the power of sustaining consciousness and being. Everything that moves is in fact moved by sex.[47]

614 ♦ As the archaic state of being is marked by androgynity, the unity of the complete man and woman—not in the physiological sense, but in the sense that the androgyne principle was awakened—; and as historicity is marked by dyogeneity, that is, dichotomy of the sexes; so will sub-historicity be marked by gynandromorphism, the intermixture of the half-man and the half-woman—again, not in the physiological sense.

615 ♦ Sexuality leads the state of bisectedness, and the duality arising as a consequence of it, into the One.

616 ♦ The essence of sexuality is the restoration of the unity of Being. Sexuality exists because the Being is broken, severed, and divided (cf. Latin *secare*: "to sever"), and this division strives to recover its unity.

617 ♦ The role of reproduction is in fact only of secondary importance when considering sex, not because it belongs to

---

[47] "In Tibetan Tantric Buddhism, the Wheel of Becoming (Sanskrit *bhāvacakra*) is generally depicted in front of a dragon representing the masculine principle, holding a tiger which represents the feminine principle in his lap in the position of sexual union. This sexual union is the motor of the whole Wheel of Becoming, that is, it keeps the Being and consciousness in motion" (András László).

something else, but because reproduction is not the actual aim of sexuality. The aim of sexuality is the restoration of unity.

618 ♦ Inwardly and in itself, the God-man is androgynous; outwardly, a man.

619 ♦ The divine man, considering his descent inwardly and in itself, is a hyper-androgyne, while in his background reality he is an androgyne, and in his foreground reality he is a man. This is because one who represents the spirit at the level of an *avatāra* in the world is *eo ipso* a man in his appearance in the world.

620 ♦ Originally, virginity did not mean asexuality, but rather abstinence from procreation. It did not mean keeping the *hymen* intact, either, but that the one possessing virginity had detached herself from the sphere of earthly becoming and risen above the level of the transmission of human life. *Virginitas* and *sexualitas* are in fact not conflicting but rather the most closely related realities.

621 ♦ The main question concerning sexuality is whether sexuality dominates me or I dominate sexuality. If sexuality dominates me, then sexuality is negative; but if I dominate sexuality, then sexuality is not negative, and indeed, under certain circumstances it might even be definitely positive.

622 ♦ Instincts do not have to be eliminated, but must be transformed into volitional forms. Analogously, the *instinctus sexualis*, the sex instinct, does not need to be eliminated, either, but must be transformed into *voluntas redunificationis*, that is, the will for reunification.

623 ♦ The mission of a man is to be entirely a man, and the duty of a woman is to be entirely a woman, inside and outside alike—at least, if they have goals which go beyond themselves. But if they do not have such aims, it does not matter what they do at all.

624 ♦ The yogi treading the path of Tantra-yoga is an *ascetic*—albeit he performs sexual exercises during the course of it.

625 ♦ If one hears of Tantra-yoga today while engaging in a life where sexuality is present, one is inclined to think that, from then on, one is following the path of Tantra. Not until now, only from now on ...

626 ♦ On the general plane of life, sexuality is a failed experiment aiming at restoration, for either it results in nothing, or it results in offspring who will not be an androgynous, but either a man or a woman.

627 ♦ It seems to be obvious that, from the union of a man and a woman, an androgyne will be born. However, experience shows us rather the opposite, even though, as the saying goes, everybody comes from a mixed marriage ...

628 ♦ At the moment of orgasm, every man becomes a woman for a moment.

629 ♦ The difference between man and woman is not a superficial phenomenon. The fact that man and woman are present as realities in the earthly-human world indicates that this has significance in the world beyond this world as well.

630 ♦ If the difference between the sexes were insignificant, there would be no sexes at all.

631 ♦ If there were no sexes at all, life would be much more practical and considerably simpler. In other words, it would be much easier if only one sex existed whose members would, in a certain period of their lives, bring forth one, two, three, or at most four offspring, and exceptionally no offspring, into the world. Accordingly, it would also be easier if life manifested itself only in its simplest form. However, it would be even simpler if life did not appear in the sphere of organic substance at all, or even better, if there were no organic substance at all, but only matter. But the simplest would be if nothing existed at all. These are the anti-hierarchies of simplicity's downward tendency.

COMBAT—WAR—HEROISM

632 ♦ One must always take the side of light to combat darkness, since allying with light means allying with one's Self.

633 ♦ The fight against darkness manifesting in the world is of essential importance. But first and foremost, I must take up the fight against the darkness in my very own soul.

634 ♦ The battle against darkness must be *omnidimensional.*

635 ♦ All things that are light-like are in solidarity with one another.

636 ♦ In actionality of the highest order, action and inaction, doing and non-doing (Chinese *wei wu wei*) coincide: this is when the non-doing becomes an act, while the doing proceeds in the serenity of non-doing.

637 ♦ (*Mors triumphalis*) To die with glory in combat is equivalent to conquering death. I was not able to conquer the enemy, but I conquered death—outwardly falling in death, but inwardly triumphing and ascending in victory and glory.

638 ♦ From a traditional perspective, offensive war is judged to be more appropriate than defensive war, since the latter is less voluntary, being waged under coercion.

639 ♦ The heroically-oriented man is *ab ovo* pacific (but not a pacifist): he not only intends to establish peace, but the ability as well—and he does it.

THINKING & INTUITION

640 ♦ Thought is important; thinking is more important; but the thinker is the most important.

641 ♦ Associative automatism, the involuntary and unconscious mental vortex, is treacherous because it is not tiring, only destructive. However, learning without conviction and interest, that can hardly be called intellectual, is only slightly better, because while it is similarly destructive, it is at least tiring.[48]

---

[48] The reason why the latter is better is that its tiring nature prevents it from continuously pervading one's waking state.

642 ♦ Problem-solving thinking is not real thinking, because it is only the *intensive degradation* of thinking. Real thinking is creative thinking: *high intensity* thinking.

643 ♦ Reflection on problems is often very concentrated thinking —however, the real subject of thinking is not I, but rather it is as if an external force concentrated my attention on the given topic. Whereas it is essential that a force should be present in my mind, it is also necessary that this force be *my* force.

644 ♦ Thinking imbued with emotionality, which is oriented toward some problem, is undoubtedly a kind of concentration, although it is not *I* who concentrates, but rather I am *concentrated*.

645 ♦ Thematic thinking is the path from swirling thoughts to supra-topical thinking.

646 ♦ Through intuition, it is always I myself whom I understand/feel.

647 ♦ The essence of intuition always refers to myself. What is understood/felt in the flash of intuition is always secondary compared to the inexpressible part of intuition which refers to myself.

648 ♦ The supreme clear intuition has no object at all. Within this intuition, man does not become conscious of anything, he simply becomes conscious.

649 ♦ The totality of *sensus* implies the duality of a Janus-face: one of its halves is comprehension and the other is feeling—but the latter not in its emotional form.[49]

650 ♦ In true intuition, the original unity of understanding and feeling is momentarily restored.

FEELING & EMOTION

651 ♦ As the original androgyne state of man has disintegrated into man and woman, so has the *sensus*, the archaic unity of comprehension and feeling, disintegrated into a degraded understanding and feeling, the latter of which has been turned into emotionality by being swept along by the *heteron* force.

652 ♦ The *dukkha* pertaining strictly to the soul is nothing other than emotionality, that is, the degenerated life and feeling of sensations.[50]

653 ♦ Emotion is diseased feeling.[51]

---

[49] The Latin *sensus* means both "comprehension" and "feeling."
[50] The Pali word *dukkha* (Sanskrit: *duḥkha*) is one of the fundamental concepts of Buddhism. Its commonest translation is "suffering," but it in fact means much more than suffering in the mundane sense: "concussion," "discomposure," "restlessness"—i.e., a state wherein man suffers something from the outside in an essential sense. Emotion, whose etymological meaning is "displacedness," means the same at the soul's level.
[51] Sense is not originally a state of commotion, for man was not the object of sense as with emotion but was rather its subject.

654 ♦ Each emotional state is a kind of obsession.

655 ♦ The supra-emotionality of feeling is restored only in exceptional moments of intuition—for intuition is always the combination of a bright and lucid comprehension and, at the same time, a supra-emotional feeling. This gives the autonomous certainty of intuition.[52]

COGNITION

656 ♦ That which Preceeds Everything cannot be known, not because it cannot be known, but because its realization, which means its attainment, is beyond all cognition.

657 ♦ The Absolute cannot be understood, not even with the most transcendent cognition.

658 ♦ What do I know? In fact, all I can know is myself. There is nothing to know where I do not know myself.

659 ♦ True understanding is self-understanding. Understanding something else is also self-understanding if it is true understanding.

---

[52] This does not necessarily imply that the content of intuition is "objectively" true.

Hierarchy

660 ◆ There is no hierarchy in the Center and from the Center, but this is much more the case with the attainment of the Center.

661 ◆ The grades manifesting in the sphere of beings are grades of withdrawal from the center of Being and the retrieval to the center of Being.

662 ◆ Being superior is equivalent to being more archaic, i.e., being closer to the *arkhé*.

663 ◆ Superiority means being close to the spirit, and being close to the spirit means being close to myself, and "being close" means that forces arising from the direct contact with myself pervade states and processes of consciousness just as they pervade the context of the Being which emerges from the states and processes of consciousness.

664 ◆ Every hierarchy is gradual, but not every gradation is hierarchical, since only those grades can be considered hierarchical which, on the one hand, constitute stages on the path leading from the sphere of general forms of being and consciousness towards transcendence, and on the other represent the stages corresponding to the path of becoming leading from transcendence towards the world *in esse*.

665 ◆ The superior precedes the inferior both essentially and temporally—but not especially in essence and not especially in time, because temporality is a mere *projection* of essentiality.

666 ♦ Superior things never originate from the inferior. Everything that comes into existence arises through the descent of the superior.

667 ♦ The hierarchy of castes: *ativarṇa brāhmaṇa*—polar and solar; *brāhmaṇa*—polar and lunar; *kṣatriya*—solar; *vaiśya*—lunar; *śūdra*—terrestrial; *pañcaka*—subterrestrial; *avarṇa*—subterrestrial and infernal.[53]

668 ♦ The advancement of a technical civilization does not measure superiority. Superiority can only be measured by its relation to the origin, beyond the origin to the beginning, and beyond this to the unbegun.

669 ♦ Each stage of existence has its level of truth.

670 ♦ Existential hierarchies correspond to hierarchies of consciousness.

---

[53] The *ativarṇa brāhmaṇa* is that arch-caste above the castes wherein the *brāhmaṇa* and *kṣatriya* castes constitute an integral union. The *brāhmaṇa* is the sacerdotal, the *kṣatriya* is the aristocratic, the *vaiśya* is the artisan-merchant, the *śūdra* is the workers' caste. The *pañcaka* ("the fifth") is the collective name for the subcastes below the castes. The *avarṇa* is the name of those without caste in the sense of subcasteness. Polarity expresses the celestial and extra-*saṁsāra*-ic origin, while solarity expresses the regal and ruling position of power of the forces of I-consciousness.

QUANTITY & QUALITY

671 ✦ No method of approach declares that quality is insignificant; but there are many views which emphatically state that quantity is what really counts and is of decisive importance.

672 ✦ The quantitative approach will emerge and gain importance as soon as the capacity to see the essence of things declines and ceases in man.

673 ✦ Quantitative aspects have no value at all, because value is *essentially* bound to quality.

674 ✦ The *potentia passiva pura* is neither quantity, nor quality—but the actuality that is transferred to the pure passive potentiality by the abandonment of its actuality in quality.

675 ✦ Each loss of quality drifts towards the nothing, because pure quantity, the *potentia passiva pura*, the *prima materia*, or the *nirguṇa mūla prakṛti* is considered nothing from the side of actuality.

676 ✦ Quantity is on the side of chaos.

677 ✦ In the cosmos—for the very reason that it is the cosmos—quantity cannot gain full control.

678 ✦ (René Guénon) If there were absolutely no qualitative difference between two beings, there would be no quantitative difference between them, either —and hence the two beings would be one being.

Body—Soul—Spirit

679 ♦ *Spiritus est regulator. Anima est mediatrix regulationis. Corpus est regulatum.*[54]

680 ♦ The spirit is not an entity, still less a substantial entity. The spirit: *subiectum in actu*—is the self-postulating Subject in action.

681 ♦ The spirit is the light of Consciousness.

682 ♦ The spirit is *subiectum in actu*—that is, the being of the Subject in action. The more it is *subiectum*, the more it is *in*, and the more it is *actu*, the more it is spirit. The spirit is ungraspable not because it is so subtle that it cannot be grasped anymore, but because it cannot be grasped in a conceptual sense either—for there is nothing palpable in it. The spirit is in fact a *relation*, and the most internal relation. The spirit is the *central* relation of the Being.

683 ♦ The true understanding in understanding is the direct presence of the spirit.

684 ♦ The spirit *qua* spirit cannot fall ill, but the relation of the spirit to the soul can fall ill. And this is *pneumatosis*.

685 ♦ There are very many people who are almost completely healthy both bodily and psychically—but who suffer at the same time from an advanced phase of pneumatosis.

---

[54] Latin: "The spirit is the ruler. The soul is the mediator of rule. The body is being ruled."

686 ♦ The notion of "spiritual soul" means that the spirit reigns in the soul. But the soul cannot be ruled by the spirit, as if the workings of the spirit operates like a state council, a parliament, or a central committee. The spirit can operate towards the soul only monarchically, like a king. He who does not realize this monarchic rule of the spirit in his soul cannot in fact be considered a human. He resembles one, but he is not one at all.

687 ♦ It is *in his soul* that man is conscious, but it is *by virtue of the spirit* that he is conscious.

688 ♦ The soul is my soul, but I am not identical with my soul. The soul is an environment; moreover, it is the closest environment of my self-postulation, that is, of the spirit. My balance, my self-control, means that I cannot allow my closest environment to become disharmonious with myself. This can be achieved in only one way: when my closest environment and circumstances do not rule over me, but if I rule over them.

689 ♦ That which is usually called inner life or the state of mind is one of the strongest antagonists of the spirit that manifests in the circus of the soul. Inner life is nothing other than the spirit—myself!—in a state of subjection to psychic activities. The self that manifests in the soul is not the subject, but the endurer of emotions.

690 ♦ The body, according to its deepest meaning, is not a substantial reality, but *a state of consciousness*—and such a state of consciousness that impounds and extinguishes all the other states of consciousness. The body is an *internal wall*.

691 ✦ The body is the denial of the spirit.

692 ✦ The body is where the spirit *qua* spirit gradually extinguishes.

693 ✦ Among the body, soul, and spirit, the body has fallen from the highest to the lowest.

694 ✦ When the body becomes unlimited, that is, when it becomes fully pervaded by the spirit to the point where it turns into consciousness, this is what the various traditions call the "resurrection of the body." The resurrection is the vanquishment of the body as body, the body as frontier.

695 ✦ The resurrection of the body is nothing other than the body's restoration into the hierarchical grade appropriate to its original rank.

696 ✦ When man turns not towards himself, but more and more towards the quantitative world, then he in fact turns towards the nothing. By losing the spirit, man kept his soul, which still had some spiritual properties. After this he kept only the body, which still has certain psychic properties, and slowly he will come to the nothing, which will only have certain bodily traits.

DEATH & IMMORTALITY

697 ✦ It is only in his exceptionally intense moments that man realizes that—putting it in the first person singular—"I will indeed die."

698 ♦ The reason why the angel of death is depicted as a skeleton is not that the skeleton outlasts everything else from the body, but that it is the body's most petrified and fossilized part, which has become the most "body": *the bone* represents the fact that the body's destiny is death. Man dies because he has body.

699 ♦ One cannot meet the angel of death because everyone carries it within his body in the form of his skeleton.

700 ♦ The relation of man living in the far-gone phase of the dark age to death is one of the most obverted: on one hand, he does not believe in his after-death subsistence, but on the other, he lives—one could say he lives so irresponsibly—as if his earthly and deeply temporal being would never end. In contrast, a spiritual man lives in a way such that he believes, knows, and experiences his own eternity both in the preexistential and postexistential sense, and yet he regards each and every day and even each moment of his earthly life as the last one.

701 ♦ Nothing better exemplifies the tragic situation of modern man than the fact that, while he considers himself completely mortal, he still lives as if he were immortal in his entirety.

702 ♦ Most people live their lives as if their bodily existence were eternal.

703 ♦ While the fact that he himself will die reveals itself to man in its fully dramatic sense during a short-term fatal disease, he does not perceive a far more certain fundamental situation: that he must, *indeed,* die.

704 ♦ Only consciousness that has already adequately dramatized death can de-dramatize it adequately.

705 ♦ Each spiritual school of high order without exception has this fundamental tenet, and without any pessimistic overtone: "Consider each day of your life as if it were the last."

706 ♦ Our whole life is necessary to prepare for the moment of death.

707 ♦ Death inevitably pertains to life as its complement. Man experiences death to the same degree that he indulges himself in life—because life contains death.

708 ♦ When life is lacking what is beyond life, then death, the complement of life, overcomes life.

709 ♦ The dissolution of consciousness after death is an individuational annihilation that is *in concreto* the annihilation of an identification; and each annihilation of an identification means the annihilation of that who/which identified himself with it.

710 ♦ While salvation and damnation provide the greatest polar tension in connection with death on the religious level, from the metaphysical point of view the tension between absolution and annihilation is the greatest.

711 ♦ Immortality is neither a faculty nor a gift, but a task to be accomplished.

712 ◆ According to the general understanding of immortality, it is the extension of a severed, particular, and isolated experience of being to infinity.

713 ◆ There are conditions under which an individual consciousness can continue to exist after the collapse of its mundane vehicles. These conditions should be gathered in the *nigredo*; conditions of the relative immortality, i.e. the conditions of *cum tempore genesis* and that of *cum tempore termination*, should be collected in the *albedo*; while the *rubedo* is the attainment of absolute immortality.[55]

714 ◆ I myself (Sanskrit *aham ātmā*) as I myself am immortal. I myself *qua* not I myself am mortal. I myself am mortal only to the extent that I am not myself.

715 ◆ I myself—as fully myself—am immortal. But as a person, or as a being connected to the physical or other subtle bodies or conditions, am, however, mortal.

716 ◆ I am immortal to the same extent as I am myself.

717 ◆ If my identification is oriented towards what belongs to the engendered world, then I will pass away together with the engendered world.

718 ◆ The reason why one is mortal is that, besides the "I-am-ness" (Sanskrit *asmitā*), one also carries 'it-is-ness' (Sanskrit *astitā*) within oneself.[56]

---

[55] Cf. the note added to the 605th aphorism.
[56] Otherness is present in man through *astitā*. The less *asmitā* is contaminated by *astitā*, the more man is immortal because the more he is himself.

719 ✦ Only the uncreated is immortal. All that is created will pass away.

720 ✦ To avoid having an end, I should relocate myself into the position where I never had a beginning.

721 ✦ Personality has a beginning, and so it has an end, too; personality is not eternal. What is eternal is the Subject, the center of the Being beyond Being.

722 ✦ Only one who realizes the state of unbegun-ness can realize absolute immortality. Only one who has no beginning can become endless.

ESCHATOLOGY

723 ✦ It is not as an award or punishment that man reaches any state after his death. Man receives not what he deserves, but that which best *corresponds* to his state.

724 ✦ The particular state one reaches after one's death is decided by that *orientation* which comprises the totality of one's mental, volitional, and affective tendencies and counter-tendencies—that which represents the entirety of being.

725 ✦ The one who chooses light is not rewarded, and the one who turns to darkness is not punished, but after death they will arrive at the condition they have been preparing for themselves during their lives.

726 ♦ The other-world is not latent, but potential: it exists through my realization. But then, the mundane world also exists in the same way...

THE BEGINNING & THE END

727 ♦ "Centrality" and "axiality" are decisive expressions of that *in se* inexpressible reality which is related to the origin in the traditional sense, to the beginning preceding this origin, and to the unbegun that is at the very root of the beginning.

728 ♦ That beginningless and the endless which contain the beginning and the end are consciousness in the most universal sense.

729 ♦ The subject is the *Alpha* and the *Ómega*. The reason why it can be the *Alpha* and the *Ómega* is that it precedes the *Alpha* and is beyond even the *Ómega*.

730 ♦ Beginning is the imprint of that which is without beginning in the world.

731 ♦ *Adam Qadmón*, "the man of the beginning," is not only the Man who arises in the beginning, but he is also the beginning of every man.[57]

---

[57] In the cabalistic Hebrew tradition, *Adam Qadmón* is the universal arch-man preceding the first man, *Adam Harisón*, the Biblical Adam.

732 ♦ (*Alétheia*) Living under the aegis of truth is equivalent to living under the aegis of awareness of the beginning.[58]

733 ♦ What should not be forgotten according to *alétheia*? The origin, the beginning, and the unbegun—that is, Myself.

734 ♦ The recovery of the origin and origin-awareness is not simply an ontological recollection in the metaphysical sense, but the return to non-oblivion.

735 ♦ The beginning and domination are principally inseparable. Only he who is in dominion can be in the beginning, and he is always in the beginning: he *always begins*. The sovereign never continues: he is in the state of eternal beginning.[59]

736 ♦ Someone who has just started to really study something could experience at the outset a profound germinal understanding within himself. This understanding is much more powerful than the understanding attained by intense study over many years. He may have been studying the topic for a long time, he knows it thoroughly, but still something is missing: what he had right at the beginning. He knew only a little about it, but somehow he understood it more deeply... This is why the study of spiritual thematics and hyper-thematics should be a process of permanent beginning. Ordinarily, man can only continue what he has start-

---

[58] The Greek word *alétheia*, denoting "truth," means in its etymological sense "non-oblivion." (Léthé is the river of oblivion in the Hades of Greek mythology.)

[59] The Greek *arkhé* or the Latin *principium* mean "beginning" and "domination" at the same time.

ed; however, the archaic understanding disappears in the process of continuation. Archaic understanding is the same as understanding something in the sense of the beginning. Thus, the real challenge is not the continuation as continuation, but the continuation as a permanent beginning, since without this, the sovereignty that characterized the beginning gradually dilutes and dies.

737 ♦ When I say that I do something in the sense of the beginning, I could say instead that I do it in a lively manner. Or I could also say that it is done by *I myself*.

738 ♦ Each world that has lost its origin-awareness is characterized by its own annihilation.

739 ♦ Everything that has a beginning is ruled over by an external force.

740 ♦ The loss of beginning is the loss of domination, and the loss of domination is the loss of beginning-awareness and origin-awareness—that is, the loss of my ultimate reality as a consciousness.

741 ♦ Everything that has a beginning passes away.[60]

DOMINATION (DOMINATIO) & POWER (POTESTAS)

742 ♦ Metaphysical traditionality does not ultimately reject anything in the world: any characteristic, any endeavor, any

---

[60] According to the Buddha's words—often quoted by András László—"Everything that has a beginning also has an ending."

attraction, any repulsion. It only rejects one thing: to lose control over anything.

743 ✦ Being superior is equivalent to being freer, more complete, and more controlled—more self-controlled; it means to be volitional with full awareness.

744 ✦ That form of being that has lost control over its own self is heading towards annihilation.

745 ✦ The more I lose myself, the more I am heading towards annihilation.

746 ✦ In the long run, all the contingencies, necessities, and regularities can only expect a decline. This is so because all that is contingent, necessary, and regular is neither voluntary, nor conscious, nor free.

747 ✦ The essence of cyclicity is not the alternation of descent and ascent, as one might think. The question of descent and ascent is merely ancillary in connection with the wholeness of cyclicity. What is fundamental in cyclicity is whether I am subject to the cycle, or if I dominate it; whether I am the moved or the mover. From a metaphysical point of view, it does not make any difference whether a movement is heading upwards or downwards.

748 ✦ The *cakravartī* is not only "the roller of the wheel," but he himself is also the wheel.[61]

---

[61] The literal meaning of the word *cakravartī* is "the roller of the wheel."

749 ♦ In most cases, the common assertion "I do what I want" demonstrates only that this is far from true. Such a one should instead say: "I do what an unidentified power—manifesting in its signs but *in se* unexperienceable—wants me to do."

750 ♦ It belongs to the nature of every being to revolt against its ruler if the latter is weak: the lion confronts its tamer if he is afraid of him, just as the demon confronts the magus if the latter is weaker than the former.

751 ♦ What is now instinct in man was originally volition.

752 ♦ All that I do not rule over works against me.[62]

753 ♦ The loss of domination entails the loss of *everything*.

Time & Eternity

754 ♦ The direction past → present → future is the direction of missed opportunities and not the direction of the process of neglecting, which is future → present → past.

755 ♦ The past is most closely connected to neglect: the reason why there is a past is that man continuously misses opportunities—he fails to collect and hold together the totality of the Being.

---

[62] This effect is not always obvious in the short term, but in the long run it inevitably manifests sooner or later.

756 ✦ The reason why there is a past is that man is not sufficiently present in the present.

757 ✦ The reason why there is temporality is that our experience of the present is not sufficiently intense. If the experience of the present were completely intense, then the temporal present would, as it were, absorb the past and the future, and time itself would disappear.

758 ✦ The future is in fact a kind of potentiality: it is from the future that things arrive, then they become the present, and if man fails to reintegrate the disintegrated Being, they become the past.

759 ✦ There are three fundamental ways to observe time: the linear view in a horizontal sense, the cyclic view, and the linear view in a vertical sense. The latter could also be called radial, since it is the concept of the breaking out of the cycle and penetrating into the timeless and motionless center.[63]

760 ✦ "The birth of the gods" and "the twilight of the gods" are a *cum tempore* beginning and a *cum tempore* ending: it happens not in time, but together with time.

761 ✦ (The hierarchical grades of infinite time) *Æternitas*: timeless, supra-temporal, absolute eternity. *Æviternitas*: endless time manifesting together with time seen from the side of timelessness. *Sempiternitas*: the endless time manifesting together with time viewed from the side of time. *Per-*

---

[63] Contemporary religious studies only know about two of these three: the linear concept in the horizontal sense, and the cyclic view.

petualitas: an endless duration. *Diuturnitas*: a finite but very long duration. *Perennitas*: that which is eternally valid, the light and imprint of *aeternitas* in time.

762 ♦ *Perennitas* is the manifestation of the absolutely supra-temporal, timeless eternity; it is the shining of *æternitas* in time, the manifestation of incorruptibility in the perishable world. *Perennitas* is eternal validity which enters and exists in the perishable world, and which represents absolute eternity.[64]

763 ♦ The *sophia perennis, religio perennis, philosophia perennis*—that is, the perennial wisdom, perennial religion, and perennial philosophy—is perennial not in the sense of being absolutely timeless, and not even in the sense of beginning and ending together with time—but in the sense that it appears in time, in the sphere of the perishable world, but it represents timeless eternity in this perishable world.

764 ♦ From the viewpoint of spirituality, it is *perpetualitas*, that is, the tendency oriented toward the realization of infinity in the world of finiteness, that has the slightest importance and validity. This is the Hegelian *schlechte Unendlichkeit*, the "bad infinity," the inadequate effort to realize infinity—quite independently of whether it is possible or not.[65]

---

[64] *Perennitas*—as the subsequent aphorism will explain—may appear as *traditio perennis, religio perennis, sophia perennis*, or *philosophia perennis*, etc.—that is, as eternally valid tradition, eternally valid religion, eternally valid wisdom, and eternally valid philosophy.
[65] Cf. *perpetuum mobile*, perpetual motion.

765 ♦ Timeless eternity is the center and ruler of the temporal world.

766 ♦ Timeless eternity (*aeternitas*) is simultaneously the supra-temporal condensation of all temporal beings. The supra-temporal contains *all*: not only that which was, but also that which will be.

767 ♦ He who could grasp the point-like nature of the present would directly step onto the path of surpassing temporality, since the basis of surpassing time is the transcendental intensification of the present.

768 ♦ The present is the gate of eternity.

Order

769 ♦ Autonomy is not the free motion of individual instincts, but the self-defined canonical order of the awakening spirit.

770 ♦ Something organic is obviously well-ordered, but it exceeds the level of sheer systems because it is not only a system, but it is a lively and spiritual coherence.

771 ♦ Every internal and external order has an organic and organically hierarchic nature. Anything without this nature is not order, but something heading towards chaos.

772 ♦ (Circum-centro-complexity) The really complex things are always complex by always being ordered around a center.

773 ♦ Since the return to the origin is possible only from ordered states, anti-traditional forces and powers primarily attack man's internal and external order so that they may create such *counter*-conditions from which the return to the origin becomes impossible, or nearly impossible.

FREEDOM

774 ♦ It is not only the *heteron*'s active exertion of power, but also its mere presence limits and contaminates freedom. If there is something that is not I, then I cannot be free in the absolute sense. Domination over others is not yet total domination. Total domination means total identity.

775 ♦ I myself am free to the very extent that I am I myself.

776 ♦ Freedom means not only the freedom of choice, but also that I can freely carry out my decision.

777 ♦ Freedom presupposes the absolute omniscience (*omniscientia absoluta*), the absolute omnipresence (*omnipresentia absoluta*), and the absolute omnipotence (*omnipotentia absoluta*). Freedom without these is not freedom. Although freedom arises from the freedom of choice, freedom does appear, but to reduce freedom to this is equivalent to a principial misunderstanding of freedom.

778 ♦ The question is not whether there is predestination or not, but whether predestination is autopredestination or heteropredestination.

779 ✦ Freedom is not indetermination, to wit, it is not an avoluntaristic or anti-voluntaristic state. Freedom is *autodetermination*: it is the state wherein I myself am determined completely by I myself. The goal is not to become undetermined, but that I myself should determine I myself.

Epilogue

780 ✦ "I am who I am" (Exodus 3:14). In other words: I was who I was, I was who I am, I was who shall be; I am who was, I am who am, I am who shall be; I shall be who I was, I shall be who I am, I shall be who I shall be—fully myself, infinitely.

Afterword

András László &
Metaphysical Traditionality

"The truly significant man, whatever he is thinking about, is actually thinking about himself."
—Otto Weininger

Exactly at that critical historical moment when modernity, becoming universal and total, was about to triumph over the traditional order of values of "ancient man," a new view appeared on the stage in the form of the "traditional school," which was not only able to salvage the values of the archaic type of man for this utterly antitraditional world, but also presented a serious intellectual challenge to modernity as a whole. What is more, even as the isolated units of Tradition were already fighting a rearguard action against the overwhelming superiority of modernity's forces, the traditional worldview—with a sudden transposition of forces to another sphere—was able to turn its ever-weakening defense into an offensive, thus proving that even if the truth of Tradition may succumb in time, by virtue of its essential atemporality it always somehow manifests itself in the temporal world. There will always be men who safeguard the sacred flame and pass it on to those who consider themselves worthy of taking it.

The traditional view and the school representing it occupies a unique position quite apart from today's plethora of views and schools, for while all the others—no matter how critical their attitude towards the present world or its particular manifestations may be—criticize and attack modernity from a platform more or less within modernity, the platform of the traditional school is free from all modernism whatsoever. Put otherwise, while all the other currents, schools, or concepts attack certain aspects of modernity from *within* modernity, the traditional school occupies a position altogether outside of modernity as a view and attitude, and aside from being formulated for modern men in the modern age, there is nothing modern about it. That is, metaphysical traditionality is alone capable of considering not only all modern phenomena, but also the totality of the modern world from without—in the sense of viewing it from above—and of measuring it against a traditional order of values whose ultimate source is the very *Metaphysicum Absolutum*: God.

Traditionality versus Modernity

Just as the life and concepts of "ancient man"—whether it be a question of pre-Columbian America, early twentieth-century Tibet, or ancient Egypt—were defined everywhere by the same essential principles, rendering the traditional world a coherent whole despite all its cultural differences, so is the modern world—independently of whether we consider today's Greece, Canada, or South Korea—defined by a similarly identical circle of principles, rendering the world an increasingly coherent whole. Indeed, between these two stable and prevailing eras lies the entire span of world history: the past centuries' ever-quickening succession of historical eras were but transitional periods, leading from prehistory in the sense of what is above history towards posthistory in the sense of what is below history.

There are various approaches and symbolisms at our disposal to formulate the difference—or more precisely, the opposition—between traditionality and modernity. First of all—following the previous train of thought—while the traditional world was branded by its principles with the stamp of *unity*, the modern world is branded by its principles with the stamp of *uniformity*. Unity is different from uniformity in that unity is realized in diversity; that is, it interlaces diversity: unity not only tolerates, but also *requires* diversity. And indeed, the traditional world was unbelievably multifarious in the cultural, religious, and doctrinal senses, and peoples living side-by-side were often separated from each other by insurmountable cultural differences. In spite of this—or in a sense, precisely because of this—those essential formative principles that resulted in the most varied applications under given circumstances were identical. The modern age, however, may not be characterized by unity for the simple reason that it gradually eliminates—and has mostly already eliminated—one of its indisputable prerequisites, namely multiplicity: no matter where one looks today, everywhere is *the same*, and the remaining differences can be attributed only to remnants of the past that have not yet been entirely eliminated. Because the principles to which the modern world has committed itself can render the world a more or less coherent unity only if at the same time they fashion the outer forms after a single model as well, and physically connect those areas that were originally not in contact with each other. Thus, modern globalism does not possess the spirit of "universality," as does the traditional world's unity, but of "generality," which is merely a poor substitute for the former. This is because the universal, not being bound to quantitative conditions, is of a qualitative nature *par excellence*; while unification, i.e., the material linking of separated parts, is only necessary where unity in principles is lacking. This demonstrates that the principles of modernity are not of the same rank as the principles of traditionality, for the former are bound to the superficial world of forms.

However, in connection with the active and operating faculty of the principles of modernity, there is another fundamental problem that cannot be left unaddressed, and which exposes not only the phenomenal "deep-rootedness" of these tenets, but also their opposition to normality. When we talk about the coherent nature of modernity, it is in fact a rather fragmentary coherence. This is necessarily so, for if modern principles were to realize perfect coherence, it would in fact lead to the modern world's total collapse. The modern world is in fact bound to apply some characteristically premodern principles—in a significantly weakened state, of course—or else it would have already broken down, and indeed—as René Guénon puts it—"in all probability it should have miserably faded away long ago." This is because a significant portion of modern tenets, being *in se* the expressions of destruction, undermine themselves when applied. Let it be enough to mention here but one characteristic feature of modernism: namely, its general relativism, which is manifested in countless areas and necessarily—but in direct opposition with modernity's intent—relativizes itself as well.

The most striking opposition between the traditional and the modern or antitraditional world can be illustrated by way of a dual linear symbolism. First of all, what is obvious at first sight is that while the former is characterized by "verticalism," the latter is characterized by "horizontalism." Tradition and the world of Tradition derive from above and adjust themselves to it. Tradition considers the peak of the hierarchy of the order of Being to be not only the Source, but the Norm and Organizing Principle as well. Indeed, since according to metaphysical Tradition the peak of the hierarchy of the order of Being is the source and norm of all things, it is at the same time the ultimate goal of all things. Source, Norm, Goal: this is what God means for Tradition. Hence, Tradition is nothing other than a vertical-principled system of dependency wherein everything adjusts itself to and endeavors for what is above it, ultimately to God. Against this "verticalism," modernity manifests as "horizontalism": expansion, conquering the world, space travel, profit, consumption, welfare, the global market, science, technology, sport, entertainment, comfort; instead of adjusting upwards, it is characterized by pragmatism, functionalism, instrumentalism, relativism, humanism, socialism—each and every one of which manifests the principle according to which "everything is measured by itself." God may very well exist, but His significance is exclusively restricted to the private domain, being neither Source, Norm, or Goal for modernity and its world.

Modernity, however, does not stop at mere horizontalism: this horizontal expansion—or rather sprawling—of the modern world serves only to conceal its continuous vertical but downwardoriented motion in the hierarchy of the order of Being. This is because the source and norm—and hence, in the sense of a dark ideality, also the goal—of antitraditional modernity is at the very bottom of the hierarchy of the order of Being, at the base of the world-pyramid. Everything derives from below, be it organic life (evolutionism) or social life (progressivism). The starting point is always primitive and inchoate. It aims at defining everything from below and strives also to adjust what is above to what is below (democratism). That which comes into being does not do so by way of descending from a higher form, as in the traditional view, but develops from a lower form. And since every "world" is prepossessed by an elementary attraction towards the form from which it derives itself—that is, towards its source—so do the innermost aspirations of the modern world point to its source: downwards. Hence, modernity's "horizontalism" is nothing other than the preparation and veiling of this "verticalism" under its negative sign and with negative tendencies—so that one can say that the intensity of the modern world's expansion is the same intensity wherewith it is continuously sliding downwards.

But from another perspective, the difference between traditionality and modernity may be approached by way of a circular symbolism. Accordingly—in the static sense—the former represents the center or the reference to the center, while the latter the periphery; or—in the kinetic sense—the former represents the *centripetal striving* towards the center, while the latter the *centrifugal drifting* towards the periphery. While the aspiration towards the center or the normative relationship with the center fuse all aspirations into an essential unity—since there is but *a single* center—the motion towards periphery has endless possibilities, and in these motions there is only one common element: moving away from the center. And while the center is the true *Principium Principiorum* of all the principles deriving from it, the "peripheral principles"—that is, the principles of modernity connected to the world of forms—necessarily represent a divergence and disintegration: attracting and leading towards endless divergence.

Moreover, if we take a rotating circle as the basis for our symbol, the center is the symbol of immobility and immutability, *motor immobilis,* and this is the same as what the archaic world represented. What is usually interpreted as archaic stasis is in fact an unbelievably dynamic force, which was more or less able to fix into stability the world that was thrown into and diffusing with time. In a river with a strong current, for example, it is not the one who surrenders to and lets himself be taken by the current who should be considered dynamic, but rather the one who is able to remain in one place *against* the current. Such an achievement is not static, but a supremely dynamic deed, even if from the outside he seems to remain in the same place. Such striving for the stability rep resented by the archaic world actually represents the permanence of eternity in the temporal world: archaic man aimed at triumphing over time via slowing down and halting time—using the direct means of the cyclical concept of time; since linear time, which is flowing away, periodically returns to the beginning and thus loses its historicity by being compelled into cycles. Modern man is also at war with time, but has chosen an utterly different strategy: he tries to overcome time not by slowing down, but rather through ever-increasing speed. The modern world's real symbol is therefore speed. Time, however, cannot be overcome by ever-increasing acceleration and speed, as is aptly demonstrated by the modern man's constant lack of time: despite his better and better time-saving devices and procedures, he remains abnormally and eternally pressed for time.

 Between the two eras, however, there is an insurmountable distance not only in the outward-manifested aspect, but in the inner aspect as well—and this is exactly metaphysics and what is most closely connected to it: spirituality. In its attempt to meet the demands of the age, the religiosity of today's man—if it can still be called religiosity at all—has sunk to a miserably low level on one hand, and has become a religiosity serving that type of man who is no longer in the least interested in transcendence; and on the other, this same scanty religion has lost its influence on man and his world to such an extent that it can practically be regarded as an appendix: the modern world's appendix, whose loss would no longer incur any kind of conflict given that it amounts to nothing more than the loss of something superfluous (which is moreover potentially dangerous). It is thus a mere ornament on the modern world's façade.

As a reaction against this "liberalised" religiosity that is gradually inclining completely towards the Earth's plane, there appeared on one hand—as a kind of "bolshevistic" distortion—a convulsive pseudo-religiosity: sectarianism, which is a grotesque counter-image of the religiosity of ancient man, of *Homo religiosus*. At the same time, another counter-effect of waning mass religiosity is the popularization, vulgarization, and in some cases perversion of the esoteric and gnostic spirituality of ancient man, that was originally open only to the most excellent—since the masses falsify these truths even by merely talking about them. On the contrary, the religiosity of ancient man appearing at the popular level not only permeated the individual himself but arranged the cultural, social, and state spheres into a true order; while at the same time its esoteric-gnostic spirituality provided the most excellent ones with the possibility of transcending the cycles and order in an upward direction, towards the attainment of freedom.

Twentieth-century metaphysical traditionality as a "philosophical school" is the repository and representative of traditional man's worldview and lifestyle. "The traditional view and the interpretation, study, and evaluation of Tradition: this is what the twentieth-century traditional school is concerned with"—says András László; because hitherto, Tradition has only been studied from a perspective alien to traditionality or even openly hostile towards it. This school completely absorbed all the essential and universal elements of ancient man's outlook, and the quintessential outlook distilled from it is what, by András László's formulation, may be called "metaphysical traditionality." Metaphysical traditionality as an outlook and school realized the synthesis of spirituality and the intellect under the aegis of traditionality—since this synthesis cannot be realized under the aegis of any other outlook than that of traditionality. The synthesis of spirituality and the intellect: precisely this is metaphysics itself—and true metaphysics, metaphysica vera cannot be but metaphysica traditionalis: traditional metaphysics. One of the outstanding representatives of this traditional school is the author of the present volume: András László.

András László

A biography consisting solely of simple facts is of some value only in the case of those who do not have much to say themselves. In other words, the more one has excelled in the realm of spirituality, the less relevant are the mundane details of one's worldly life. Naturally, this applies to András László as well.

András László was born in Budapest in 1941. After graduating from high school, he read Calvinist theology, but no sooner had he begun than he was forced to terminate his studies because he was arrested. The original charge of "playing an initiating and leading role in a plot to overthrow the people's democratic political system" was subsequently greatly reduced, so he was imprisoned for only four months. In the meantime, as early as 1959 he had contacted the only legal Hungarian organization that could satisfy the interests of those who wished for more than mere theology: the Buddhist Mission. First only as a student, and then between 1964 and 1968 also as a lecturer, he was active at the Kőrösi Csoma Sándor Buddhist Seminary (later renamed the Institute of Buddhology) which operated within the Mission's frame. It was during this period that he became acquainted with Béla Hamvas, the first thinker to introduce the Traditional school to Hungary, and for five years, until Hamvas' death in 1968, they engaged in a friendly and spiritually fruitful relationship.

For both Hamvas and his young disciple, however, the sixties proved to be a trying decade from an existential point of view. László, for his part, had a succession of some twenty jobs from the *Éttermi és Büfé Vállalat* (Catering and Buffet Company) to the *Aszfaltútépítő Vállalat* (Asphalt Road Construction Company), and from store house handyman to truck security guard. In the meantime he once again tried to continue with the study of Calvinist theology, but because he disliked the atmosphere prevailing there, he switched to Catholic theology before completing his first year. As a lay student, he finished the usual six-year curriculum in four years, between 1971 and 1975. He also kept in touch with the Buddhist Mission: in 1975 he obtained his doctoral degree from the Mission's West German Priory with his dissertation, *Licht des Alls in Menschenwesen* (The Light of the All in Man), the Hungarian version of which was published in the same year under the title *A mindenség fénye az emberben*. After his doctorate, he became a full professor at the Institute of Buddhology, where he taught the philosophy of religion—

which meant in fact lecturing on the traditional *Weltanschauung*—until 1983. In that year he broke contact with the Mission, and from then on he began giving lectures—at first only in private apartments. After 1988, the changing political situation enabled him to give public lectures and seminars to present his ideas.

In Budapest, Szentendre, Sopron, Nagycenk, Debrecen, and Nyíregyháza—to mention only a few—he held and continues to hold lectures on nearly all the problems and questions that are indispensable for one's essential knowledge and orientation, be it the relationship between Being and consciousness from the viewpoint of Oriental metaphysical traditions; the cosmic and metaphysical origin of man and his anthropological structure; the questions of death and immortality; the interrelationship between cognition and action; the problems of transmuting cognition as a faculty of consciousness; the conceptual foundations of metaphysical praxis; the problems of spiritual deviations; the study of the modernity's multifarious aspects in connection with religion, culture, science, society, lifestyle, and faculties of consciousness; the relationship between Rightism and traditionality; the connections between freedom, democracy, and liberalism; the relationship between society and state, faith and knowledge; Tantric yoga; the metaphysics of sexuality; the relationship between Christianity and universal Tradition; the relationship between a crisis of consciousness and the world crisis; the metatheology of Sophia and the Logos; the traditional concept of art; the metaphysical foundations of Buddhism; the path from supra-historicity through historicity towards sub-historicity; and the problems of time and eternity in connection with metaphysical theory and praxis.

Solipsism—Kali-Yuga—Rightism

András László's traditional *Weltanschauung* has three key concepts: "solipsism"; the *kali-yuga*, or the dark age; and "Rightism."

"Solipsism" sounds rather unpleasant in the history of European ideas, being composed of the Latin *solum* (only) and *ipsum* ([my]self). In fact, there are several kinds of solipsism, but all originate in two basic types: ethical solipsism and ontological solipsism—or, to use another approach, practical solipsism and theoretical solipsism. While ethical-practical solipsism covers a sort of extreme egoism, ontological-theoretical solipsism—starting from the epistemological observation that everything existing or apparently existing is verified by experience—arrives at the conclusion that the empirical world exists only in experience, *ergo* in the experiencing subject.

What connects the two versions of solipsism—and at the same time separates them from András László's solipsism—is that the subject of both is the individual, while the subject of metaphysical solipsism is not the self-confined individual, but the *Individuum Absolutum*, in which the *individuum separatum* is rooted. This final, universal Subject—that ultimately, I myself am—is in fact God Himself: that is, God is the final Subject of each and every subject, and it is only through this Subject that every subject is a subject in its own, particular form. Thus, an equality sign appears between God and Myself in the ultimate sense, God and Myself being related to each other as in the corpuscular and the wave-like nature of electrons in microphysics: how we call it depends on the particular way of contemplation. As Meister Eckhart put it: "... those eyes with which I can see God are the same eyes through which God sees me. My eyes and God's eyes are the same—one vision, one cognition, one love."

Hence, it is not only that—putting it in the first person singular—God is after all the ultimate, only real Ego of my own being, but that my actual Self is in fact the God of my present particular identifications. This is the peculiar situation that prompted King Śikhidhvaja in the *Yoga Vāsiṣṭha* to make the following paradoxical statement: "I respectfully bow my head before my own true Self." However, this means not only that the roots of God and the individual coincide (autotheism), but that at the same time there is only one Being, the being of this Absolutum, and it would be absurd to propound any being beyond this being ([theo]monism): "The true being—that is, God's being—is such being that appears as non-being, while the imaginary being—that is, the being of the world—is such non-being that appears as being," says the Sufi 'Azīz Nasafī, exactly in the same sense as it was expressed by Plato, according to whom the former "forever exists, and has nothing to do with becoming," while the latter "is ceaselessly becoming, but never exists." Thus, solipsism is the logical conclusion of the coexistence of autotheism and (theo)monism—and András László condensed this conclusion into the following quintessentially terse and clear definition: "Every *heteron* ('other') is non-recognized *auton* ('myself')."

It goes without saying that, under such circumstances, there is no question of egoism, nor even of *un*selfishness as conventionally interpreted. After all, as Ramaṇa Maharṣi puts it, "... if one were to recognize the truth that everything he gives to others he actually gives to himself, what would become of moral men, what of those who help others? As everybody is identical with one's own ultimate Self, whatever one does to somebody, he actually does to himself."

This additionally clarifies that metaphysical solipsism is not merely a question of philosophical outlook, and not simply a matter of intellectual comprehension, but a *living experience* obtainable by the consummation of the metaphysical path, and this same experience is the source of all those metaphysical schools—from Hindu *advaita vedānta* to Buddhist *vajrayāna* to the Muslim *wujūdī*-school to Greek and Christian Neoplatonism—that asserted, either implicitly or explicitly, the concept of solipsism.

There is one point, however, that lends a quite special and unique flavour to András László's theory of solipsism, and this is the special significance of the *own person*—my personal and individual self-awareness, which cannot be multiplied. It is significant because the various forms of philosophical solipsism universally adopted (and adopt) the view that the other person has the same right to solipsistically see and interpret the world as the given solipsist—that is, solipsism as view and reality has several subjects. Clearly, only in a very relative sense can such a solipsism be considered solipsism, since it postulates more than one *ipsum*—or rather *ipsus/ipse* and *ipsa* (masculine and feminine *ipsum*)—and hence, solipsism would be hurt in each and every person's case; that is, each and every person would as it were be punching a hole in the balloon of solipsism through which its air would be continuously escaping.

In contrast to philosophical solipsism, the metaphysical solipsism of the traditions certainly did not make this mistake, yet it was András László who, by introducing the notion of the "own person," definitively clarified the connection between the person(s) and the Universal Subject. The own person is not simply one person among many, but fundamentally differs from all the other persons. This is not so in the sense that this person is mine, while all the other persons are not mine but each belongs to someone else (since in this case there would be as many own persons as persons, only with the subject of their ownness being different in each case); but in the sense that all the other persons are rooted in the own person, and it is through the own person that they are rooted in the ultimate Subject of being.

Thus, in contrast to the multitude of persons, there is but one own person—or, in other words, there is but one I: "mine"; any other "I" is in fact not I but you or he—to wit, it is *heteron* (that is of course non-recognized *auton*). Like these other persons, the own person is also part of *māyā*, the universal enchantedness, but that particular part through which the whole of manifestation, together with all the persons—though not according to their own identification (cf. aphorism 290)—may return to Themselves/Myself (*ātmā*). And as in every dream, the dream-world and its characters are after all emitted and created by the dreamer himself, but this emanation is effected by the dreamer's dreaming self— that is, the dreaming own person—and awakening can only occur after the dream-world and its characters integrate into one of the persons participating in the dream: the same dreaming own person. This is also true of the waking world together with its numberless persons generated through the own person—*my* own person—and through the own person does it return to that source from which it ultimately originated. Thus, the own person both in the individual dream-world and in the universal enchantment of Being—acquires a quite unique significance, and it is easy to see that the solipsistic theory in its entirety invokes such a metaphysical practice whose essence is the *reductio* in the original sense of the word—that is, leading back. This is because he who wants to awaken must come to Himself, and once you have come back to Yourself, everything will return to you.

The second cardinal point in András László's *Weltanschauung* is the *kali-yuga*, the present dark age, or in a wider sense the doctrine of cyclic descent. The standpoint of metaphysical Tradition is that history is characterized by a continuous decline, and that this decline has recently reached its nadir. The reason for the decline lies in the superiority of the beginning; and the reason for the superiority of the beginning is the superiority of the Source, that is, God—for the farther something gets essentially and ontically from its ultimate Source, the Non-manifested Manifestor, the lower it descends. Hence, decline is a universal *law of Being* which pertains just as much to the totality of the world of becoming as to each of its particulars (for sooner or later everything perishes, deteriorates, disintegrates ...); and against which free and conscious will alone might initiate a countermove. This is the reason why Tradition turns *in the direction of* the past: not *to* the past, but *through* the past to the Source, for Tradition regards not that which is old as the norm, but perceives the norm manifesting in the old. It goes without saying that modern men radically refuse this concept—and it is the refusal of this same concept that makes them modern. This is because the essence of modernity is antitraditionality, that is opposition to Tradition, and the basis of this agressive praxis is the theory that "the old" is necessarily less valuable than "the new." This approach—that is, the irrational belief in evolution and progress—is in fact *structurally* atheistic because it implies that the beginning is inferior, and thus if there were something that was the source of the beginning, it would be even more inferior. The logical correlate—or, rather, counter-image—of the *Metaphysicum Absolutum*

of Tradition is therefore the hypothetic *Physicum Nihilum* of modernity, that is the substantial root of our world, the *materia prima*, the *potentia passiva pura*. The god of modernity is Nothingness.

When modern man says, "How can we speak about descent when the modern age has witnessed incredible progress with respect to both science and technology?", by this same assertion he proves what he wanted to refute: for he regards mere material development (science, technology) as the standard for human progress; that is, he regards as a standard something purely instrumental, which in turn acquires its value only from that purpose whose instrument it is. Therefore, progress in the modern sense cannot be considered anything other than a *satisfaction of increasingly inferior needs in an increasingly superior way*—and, as Béla Hamvas puts it, "… if we spiritually valorize a hundred-seat jet plane, we have to concede that it is worth no more than a merry-go-round. Rather less."

It is certainly not our business to question progress in the fields of science and technology, but the traditional school treats these same fields as something of an inferior order with respect to the true object of mankind, and hence it does not grant them a crucial role in deciding the question of progress. This is because the real object of mankind is not horizontal expansion in human existence, but the vertical transcending of human existence: developing from the human towards the suprahuman and the divine—and society should be ordered according to such principles as do not hinder the individual's vertical existential development, but support it. On the contrary, modern man—to quote Werner Heisenberg—increasingly resembles the ship whose compass no longer points towards the North Pole, but towards its own "iron hull" (cf. humanism)—and we know that for

Tradition the North Pole, the boreal region, and the North Star representing the hyperboreal region with its immobility and axiality represent that same extra-*saṁsāra*ic Archimedean fulcrum whereby the world can indeed be turned inside out.

This is not the only field that demonstrates permanent descent. There is another field as well that exerts even more influence than scientific and technical achievements on contemporary man's views and existential level (which is often inversely proportional to the standards of living)—and this is culture. It goes without saying that the value of culture cannot be defined by quantitative criteria: How many books does an average individual read yearly? How many theater performances can he afford? How many television channels can he access?—and so on. The value of culture—together with the cultural level of a given age—is defined by that inherent quality which dominantly characterizes the culture, and which inevitably brands the whole of society. If we examine the dominant influence of culture, we can obviously disregard that insignificant minority that chooses on the basis of superior criteria what they allow to play a role in their lives; we can disregard it all the more because the overwhelming majority of the cultural intelligentsia do *not* even belong in this category!

The decisive word is on the side of mass culture. Mass culture is a consumption-oriented ancillary culture, and this fact alone suffices to characterize its general *level* on one hand and its general *tendency* on the other. In this mass culture that strives to satisfy all levels of demand, even the cultural simpleton feeds on *essentially* the same things as the connoisseur, even if an almost unbridgeable distance separates these two cultural levels in the mode of formulation and in fastidiousness. For while the "popular" version of mass culture, that appeals to the lowest instincts, oscillates between stone-hard brutality and mawkish sentimentality—taking much care, of course, to always accomodate some form of sin or crime—the "high" version of the same in almost all its manifestations suggests the unreality, the non-existence, and the absurdity of the counter-world and counter-values of the world depicted by the "popular" version—and this with increasing efficacy, and at the same time and in some sense with increasingly firmer grounding. Since modern man does not know the *beautiful* and the *noble* in the classical sense of the words (because indeed, these cannot be accomodated in the pragmatical consumer-information world any longer), starting from himself he believes that such values in fact do not even exist, and have never existed, and descriptions informing us about such things in connection with past ages are nothing but fairy tales.

It is obvious that a consumption-oriented ancillary culture cannot fulfil the *normal* function of culture: it cannot be a *preserving* culture. On the contrary, it necessarily generates continuous inflation. And for those who are able to survey the cultural tendencies of millennia from above, there can hardly be any doubt that while archaic-traditional culture and art was of an *exalting* character, and the ensuing culture and art of a *reflective* character, modern and especially postmodern culture and art are already of a *destructive* character—and not only in their popular manifestations, but often even when their most excellent productions are considered.

The third point that is highly significant in András László's philosophy and must therefore be touched upon is *Right-*

ism. Traditionality is a complex *Weltanschauung* covering all aspects and levels of human existence—yet, it can be said that Tradition as the worldview of ancient man, and traditionality as the concept of contemporary anti-modern men, has two pillars. The first is *spirituality*, that is the instrument, method, and path that enables man's self-transcendence towards his own ultimate divine totality; and *politics* taken in the broadest sense, that is the organization of people into hierarchical social and governmental structures. While the former is marked by Freedom, given that its ultimate aim is to transcend all conditional bonds, i.e. that man recognize himself as the *Absolutum*, the unconditional totality of being; the latter is marked by Order, the terrestrial reflection and image of the celestial world whose role is to secure such a *frame* for the human world, both at the collective and individual level, that enables life to harmonize with divine principles. The terrestrial Order must in all respects adapt itself harmoniously to the celestial Order; or in other words, the normative goal of society or the collective must always coincide with the normative goal of the individual. And this is indeed always the case: for just as the sacred pervades everything in the ideal traditional society, so does consumption pervade everything in the "ideal" modern society.

In the archaic era, or generally speaking in the age of Tradition, man *lived* spontaneously, as it were, and without any sort of objectification according to what might be called Rightism in the original sense of the word. By contrast, Leftism in today's sense of the word is hardly older than a few hundred years: it first appeared in the late period of Tradition's disintegration to become increasingly dominant since its appearance in the form of a gradual leftward drift of the relative and actual political center (the absolute center, of course, never changes). This leftward drift is still in progress today—in spite of the fact that all notable political parties today are almost exclusively Leftist. That which is considered Rightism today, or the party which defines itself as Rightist, can only be considered Rightist from the traditional point of view in a very relative sense. This pertains not only to today's parliamentary Rightism and extreme Rightism, but also to those extreme Rightist movements of the first half of the twentieth century, since they were—and still are—if not the same, contaminated with Leftist ideas to such an extent that if we were to designate their place between the absolute Right and the absolute Left, they would all be closer to the Left extremity than to the midpoint between the two extremities, that is the absolute center (cf. illustration below).

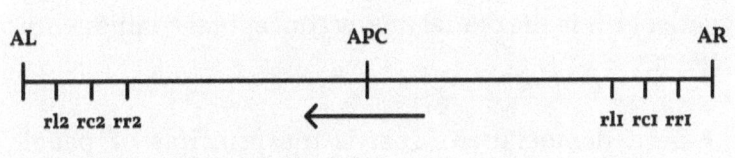

The relationship between absolute rightism and leftism and relative rightism and leftism.
AR: *absolute rightism* / **APC**: *absolute political center* / **AL**: *absolute leftism*. **rr1**: *relative rightism in the early period of the disintegration of Tradition* / **rc1**: *relative center in the early period of the disintegration of Tradition* / **rl1**: *relative leftism in the early period of the disintegration of Tradition*. **rr2**: *relative rightism today* / **rc2**: *relative center today* / **rl2**: *relative leftism today*.
The arrow indicates the direction of the drift of the relative center through history.

That which is Rightism in the traditional sense cannot therefore be identified with what is called "Rightism" today—and not because it is less, but because it is *much more* Rightist: *maximal Rightism uncontaminated by Leftist ideas.* This is because Rightism does not belong to those qualities and values that are ideal when optimal, but to those that are ideal when maximal. Hence, the term "extreme Rightism" is in fact *contradictio in adiecto*, because Rightism has and may have no extreme variation, due to the fact that something can only have extreme variations when it possesses an optimum point and then swings over that point. What is called "extreme Rightism" today, *if it is extremist in any sense at all*, is extremist not because of its Rightism—that is, not because it overrepresents Rightist values—but because of other reasons (aggressive anti-Leftism, violence, populism, demagogy, etc.).

What are the criteria of *maximal* Rightism? Putting it negatively, it is the denial of any conceptual components of Leftism,

* be it democratism, that is the principle of people's sovereignty that realizes the reign of quantity in the social sphere, and which may manifest in the form of bourgeois democracy ("mob rule," as Plato puts it) just as well as Communist dictatorship (which, owing to its inefficiency and, with respect to the former, all but conservative nature, was bound to disappear from the political arena);
* be it socialism, which is none other than humanism at the social level, that is a kind of "social narcissism" when society focuses on itself;
* be it nationalism and internationalism, which represent successive degrees for the disintegration of the old order and the establishment of a new counter-order;

♦ be it egalitarianism, which disqualifies individuals (i.e., deprives individuals of their qualities); or liberalism, the theory and practice of the universal deprivation of values and ideas that, while announcing free competition among ideas, reserves the position of a superordinate director for itself;

♦ be it revolutionary ideology, whose fundamental tenet is that if two factors are hierarchically arranged one below the other, then the one in the higher position will necessarily oppress, abuse, and exploit the subordinate one, whereas the latter must resort to "revolutionary violence" in order to shake off the former's yoke;

♦ be it relativism appearing at numberless levels and in numberless forms, this *saṁsāra*ic concept *par excellence*, which strives to render every truth—save its own—relative; be it relativism, this par excellence samsarian theory, which aims at making every truth relative, except its own;

♦ be it rationalism, which arises when the merely instrumental and essentially executive intellectual factulty, reason (*ratio*), which knows only the question "how?", shakes off the "shackles" of the supra-rational intellect (*intellectus*), which always considers the particular in relation to the whole, and which alone is competent in the questions " what?" and "why?"; and either becomes independent or outright enters the service of subrational powers;

♦ be it secularized messianism, that is utopianism (inseparable from both forms of th Left-wing attitude), which the more systematically it works for the sake of the "Sacred Goal," the more it tries to conceal the actual nature of "the end of history" and the woeful role it assigns to the "last man" in it;

♦ be it that self-service religiosity which, instead of lifting man up,continually degrades the level of religion;

♦ or be it the squirrels-wheel of production and consumption, the only cycle known to modern man, and that is forced to move at an ever more furious pace.

Finally, we must not forget that both basic forms of Leftism go hand-in-hand with both materialism as a dogmatic ideology (social democracy) and materialism as mentality (liberalism).

Moreover, Leftism manifests at the psychological level as well, for while today everything aims at liberating the instincts and installing them in a dominant position, at halting the inhibitions, and at continuously increasing desires in order to seek ever-newer satisfactions, then what happens is nothing less than what is supposed to remain below and in confinement being allowed to well up and rule. (For a modern Leftist post-Freudian person, one of the most frightening words is "repression.") This principle, having become the basis of twentieth-century psychology, is but the intrusion of Leftism into the sphere of psychology. Leftism in all cases makes the most of that political conjuncture whose orientation is determined by the *kali-yuga*—meaning that it does not direct changes, as pretended by certain of its theoreticians (Friedrich A. Hayek, for instance), but it merely serves a blind mechanism. Generally speaking, Leftism—at least in its liberal, by this time solely progressive variation—prefers things to *be organized by themselves,* and to let them loose within certain relaxed confines ("self-regulating systems," *laissez faire*), which of course results in continuous inflation, levelling, and loss of values in all fields, be it economics, culture, religion, and so on. If, however, this process is not sufficiently rapid, or if the given category has already reached its natural existential level and cannot be expected to decay any further by itself, Leftism strives to "organize"—rather disorganize!—them according to such principles as are beneath them, and in so doing foster their further lowering.

Putting it positively, pure Rightism proceeds from a world-concept that has God at its summit, and through analogies, projections, or mappings, it strives to *organize* every sphere of life so as to be in harmony with this *Principium Principiorum* (cf. "[thy will be done] on Earth as it is in Heaven"). It always adjusts the lower to the higher, and the higher to what is higher still, continuing up to the Supreme, who *ultimately* determines everything. Thus, Rightism is theocratic by principle, and this divine dominion can only be realized through monarchical and aristocratic (feudal) institutions. At the juncture of Heaven and Earth stands the King, the man *par excellence*, in whom being a man, interpreted not as an endowment but as a possibility, is fully realized, and who is the embodiment of that central principle which, pervading the whole world "under Heaven," specifically manifests everywhere according to the domain in question. Rightism does not separate the Church and the State—in other words, the profane and the sacred spheres—because essentially they essentialy both point towards the same ultimate Point from which they originate.

The fundamental slogan of the Rightist establishment in traditional society has therefore always been Order—and Order always organizing on the basis of a higher principle, a higher organizing precept (Sanskrit *dharma*). Tradition has always been aware of the fact that what the people or the masses need is not freedom, but Order. As José Ortega y Gasset excellently pointed out, it is *inertia*, and not numerical majority, that makes the mass the mass. The mass is what can always be be "mobilized." Knowing that, Tradition has essentially always been conscious of the fact that the people and the masses, being inert and consequently apt to sink, must be *controlled from above*. Obviously, if the maintaining power of Order weakens or ceases, the mass starts sinking because of the inertial force of its own weight (this is the "power" of the people: its own inertial momentum). This is why traditional people, on encountering secular culture and civilization, almost immediately start to decline and are finally ruined, because the bonds that have always held them relatively high up, break. But this mere "releasedness," which was a characteristic of the transitional period between traditionality and modernity, has been supplemented with the activation of special degrading forces in the modern, and particularly in the postmodern, era.

This certainly does not mean that the traditional world rejected freedom. On the contrary, *only* the traditional world held freedom in the true dignity becoming to its rank. Freedom, as an ability and virtue, was the privilege of the few—of the excellent—while Order was everyone's task. "Ancient man" was aware of the fact that Freedom cannot be democratized, for *virtus* in the original sense of the word—a virile virtue attached to high qualities—cannot be meted out, so to speak. Freedom is no endowment to be provided for people but an ability to be achieved. Neither the trade union, nor the Parliament, nor the women's rights movement can obtain freedom for anyone—because the freedom they secure is never actual freedom. It is the servant who needs to be liberated, and a servant liberated remains a servant: a liberated servant. Only the *victor* is free; only the one who is able to rule—and first of all, who is able to rule *over himself!* Just as every cognition has self-knowledge as its basis, so does every type of control have self-control as its basis and consummation. Besides Freedom, control is closely related to Order as well: that is, the choosing of Order already points towards Freedom, and is an important step towards Freedom—for Freedom can only be achieved through Order and through surpassing the consummate, maximalized Order. It would be preposterous to assume that freedom might be realized without *strength* and *power*—to wit, *personal* strength and *personal* power. Likewise, it would be unreasonable to believe that any but the superior can be free; the inferior, for the very reason that it is—even in the prime of its political power—always *below*, can never be free. Only that one can be free who is above, and ruling is possible only from above.

What the modern Leftist/liberal masses consider to be freedom is no freedom at all, but mere liberation and breaking loose: *emantipatio*. These are not the result of personal power and victory, but of a loss of restraints—which indeed can be carried out even by an external institution. Freedom requires strength; breaking loose, on the contrary, requires only weakness and absence of control. The mass cannot maintain itself, because such maintenance always requires an inner controlling power; it never holds itself up, but is held up from above: by nature, it lets itself go. Therefore, when the controlling and maintaining power of Order ceases, the mass ends up in the state of being uncontrolled. This is what liberation and breaking loose mean. The mass feels free only when it is released from above, and then it can at last abandon itself to the down-pulling force of its own weight, the ontological gravitation always acting upwards from below, and pulls down what is above. The freedom of the mass is therefore not the freedom of the man who has overcome his own force of inertia so that he can ascend freely, but that of a man in freefall. Thus, what is glorified as freedom today is the diametrical—and, at the same time, *parodic*—counter-image of actual freedom.

As Julius Evola has astutely observed, the modern Leftist has an essential affinity for slavery and an aversion to actual freedom. This is clearly demonstrated by the fact that past ages are today regarded as ages of the yoke and servility for the simple reason that modern man identifies himself with the inferior ones and not with the free lords. And with surprising candour, the same has also been asserted by the celebrated theoretician of modern democracy, Francis Fukuyama, according to whom today's liberal citizen is the spiritual descendant of the liberated slave—as can easily be detected in the "venality coupled with slave mentality" (Plato) of the modern democratized mass-man. The fact that it is not freedom which pervades the modern man's form of life can also be clearly seen in his identification of "freedom" almost exclusively with freedom of choice or—in political terms—with free elections. This is because freedom of choice—whether it concerns political parties, products, or holiday resorts—is in most cases only means the choice that holds the greatest allure for people. In other words, in freedom of choice, man can "freely" choose the thing that is most attractive to him. As for "free" elections, the average man will almost always choose the greater slavery over the lesser one. The deluded masses "have their own desires: they invariably stick to the ideology by which they have been subdued," according to Theodor W. Adorno, who certainly cannot be "accused" of Rightist sympathies. It cannot be called freedom when man merely yields to the strongest, most attractive choice among several others. Freedom of choice is therefore nothing more than the choice of that which is apparently the most favourable among the available possibilities—while a truly free choice should choose not only from among the offered alternatives, but one should also ready to reject the offered choices in order to create new ones.

The free choice of homonculi produced on the assembly line by the modern liberal ideology hardly surpasses the free choice of those who may—freely—choose between a thirty-day prison sentence and a thousand-dollar fine. And as for political elections, the control of processes in a liberal democracy is not in the hands of the parties and politicians representing the face, or so to say *persona* of politics, and are bestowed with very little freedom of movement. It is in the hands of powers behind the scenes, that often remain hidden—be they interest groups of varying rank and degree that are outside the parties and yet enforce their will "from above," or be they the so-called "opinion makers" who do the same from below, by shaping public opinion. These therefore render those "democratic elections" a mere show that is intended to maintain the illusion of the disenfranchised man's freedom.

Thus, in the modern liberal world, freedom is all but unknown, since it is precisely freedom that only rarely becomes an issue at all. Man does not choose freedom, but whether he will get suntanned in Tahiti or Haiti by the Sun of God; whether he will drive a Mercedes or a Volvo; whether this or that political party will provide him with greater welfare—and so on. In short, he does not choose freedom against slavery, the lesser slavery against the greater one, or the greater freedom against the lesser one—but rather only that which he believes will satisfy his increasingly material desires and embeds him more and more deeply in the "being serviced = being at someone else's mercy" system of dependency.

Actually, the problem is not that free elections are the freedom to choose among the "lords" (and usually, that "lord" gets elected who binds the "elector" to even deeper servility and thus enslaves him yet more), but that what came to master the voter through his election should rather serve him. One manifestation of this process is, as Gábor Czakó puts it, when man "proceeds" from subjugation to people to subjugation to things; or when, according to Adorno, he replaces the endowing of things with souls (animism) with making souls into things (industrialism). Zeno of Citium, the founder of the Stoic school, classified people—as opposed to the horizontal psychological typologies—along a *vertical*, that is, qualitative typology, and into two groups: the group of the worthless and that of the able, or, according to another translation, as the vulgar or the excellent.

And who are the worthless? In modern times the infallible sign of worthlessness is when one—rebelling against the tension between his own actual state and any superior state or possibility—he contests, lies against, and "misinterprets" the higher state's superiority, lowering it to his own level (and hence depriving himself of the very possibility of ascending higher). In ancient times, the worthless—by this also proving their superiority to their modern successors—were quite able to live with this tension and their own inertia that prevented their ascending higher, but the modern worthless, proceeding from their democratic "dignity" (cf. *"Dignity for all!"*) and exercising a special form of the old revolutionary violence, pull all they can see above themselves down to their own level. But the real nature of worthlessness and vulgarity is exposed simply when comparing it to ableness: the able are not those who are experts in this or that, be it arts, crafts, or sports—but who are able and excellent in surpassing themselves *ad indefinitum*; indeed, *ad infinitum*. In short, the able are those who are able to win complete freedom for themselves. It is they who are spoken of by that glorious guide-of-the-river-ford, the Arrived, the Buddha: "Look at the happiness of the Arhats! There is no trace of desire left in them. They have hewn out the thought of 'I am' and torn asunder the net of illusion. They are motionless, beginningless, immaculate, real Persons; they are those who have become God, great heroes, and sons of Awareness; they are steadfast in all situations, free from the compulsion of reincarnation; they stand above their conquered 'ego,' they have won their own battle in the world, and they voice the 'lion's roar.' The Awakened are truly incomparable."

But is there any hope, not just of reaching freedom and surpassing oneself, but simply of surpassing one's own vulgarity as one vulgarizes himself alongside millions of others every day? And is there a more effective means of vulgarizing oneself than by watching, listening to, reading, and doing the same as they do; that is, by accepting the same cultural nourishment as hundreds and hundreds of thousands of others?

Modern spirituality strays onto a very dangerous path if it is averse to and even looks down on all politics, feeling that spirituality and politics, the spirit and power are incompatible. This is because apoliticism—unless the undifferentiated denial of the political is preceded by a sharp differentiation (cf. aphorism 445)—almost inevitably leads to surrendering to the prevailing political background radiation. In the present historical moment in Hungary, this means the aggressive extreme-liberal "undifferentiationism" that aims at the disintegration of all values, and which permits radicalism only for its own use, hence depriving all other views of their own *radix*, of their own root, and at the same time of an authentic connection with their own source (which always results in the slow withering of the given organism). It goes without saying that the spirituality arising under the aegis of this particular political background radiation will completely bear the stamp of its characteristics—and in so doing will lose all those characteristics that made spirituality what it was in the traditional era, and which make it what it is under all circumstances. Accordingly, the man of modern pseudo-spirituality, instead of choosing a heroic spiritual battle, will instead surrender himself to the suction of obscure and intangible powers, and instead of aspiring for the higher, he gives himself up to something—to what exactly, he does not quite know himself. It is therefore not at all surprising that "meditation" in this thoroughly unmanly, self-service consumer-spirituality is not the "battle royal" (Ramaṇa Maharṣi) of ancient man treading the spiritual path, but is in fact considered *relaxation*. The "glory" of the modern age is that it has rendered meditation, which was once the privileged practice of the most prominent people, as one of the mental forms of relaxation available to anyone. And we know only too well that when a thoroughly materialistic—*heavy-grown!*—man, having been torn away from his higher, sustaining existential contexts *by others*, "lets himself go" according to the directive of Leftism appearing in the spiritual domain, then only the lowest point can set a limit to his sinking.

The Maxims

The meaning and true depth of András László's maxims in their fullest extent may unfold only gradually before the reader; and as the first aphorism puts it, this is possible only for those who belong to those fortunate few whose eyes are covered with only slight dust. But those whose eyes are thickly covered with dust will necessarily find these maxims either incomprehensible, meaningless, or uninteresting.

And there will certainly be some—and perhaps not even a few—who will think that they do not need these sorts of thoughts for the reason that their eyes are not covered by dust at all...
What does it mean, that this book speaks only to those whose eyes are covered but with slight dust? András László represents the *complete metamorphosis* of thinking and of the Being-concept, because this is the fundamental condition for the thinker's and beholder's—that is, the subject's—complete metamorphosis. Only the potential spiritual elite, the number of which should be low according to the law of quality–quantity reciprocity, can accomplish this. Moreover, since the metaphysics represented by András László is built on the synthesis of spirituality and intellectuality, the *spiritus* and *intellectus*, besides the spiritual orientation, it presupposes serious intellectual abilities—and even considerable inclination towards gnosis—besides a spiritual orientation. For while spirit without intellect necessarily proceeds towards the path of least resistance, towards either sentimental moralism or pseudo-esoteric deviation, intellect without spirit is bereft of all normative—upward-pointing—orientation. Indeed, exactly those open towards the various flattened or distorted forms of spirituality—be it the spirituality of the church, which tends towards sentimentalism in most cases; cheap New Age-type "esoteric spirituality"; or Westernised forms of Far-Eastern religions drowning in either moralism or pseudo-esoterism—are almost without exception the victims of an intellectual minimalism. Without a symbiosis of spirituality and intellectuality—and a symbiosis arising under the aegis of traditionality—one hardly stands a chance of belonging, not only in a potential but also in an actual sense, to that category of nobility that according to

Ortega is nothing other than the "constant aptitude for surpassing oneself."

In the case of one whose eyes are thickly covered with dust, it is not that he does not see *something*, and not that he displays blindness towards some sort of spiritual teaching—but rather towards his own self: towards the metaphysical importance of himself. Such a man is measured by *himself* and found wanting. He does not take *Himself* seriously because he cannot see the wholeness of his life—or from a different perspective, because he considers it a set of more or less accidental incidents—he does not regard his life as a spiritual task. This is just what the Parable of Talents emphasizes: when the master returns and calls his slave to account for what he accomplished with the borrowed talents, he will ask not—as the parable's secular interpretation assumes—how the metaphysically unimportant talents have been put to use in the various fields of life, but only about the use of the only true, central talent: how one's ability for permanent self-overcoming has been developed.

Closely connected to this is one of the striking characteristics of András László's maxims: they are often formulated in the first person singular. The importance of this cannot be exaggerated. Besides the fact that certain things cannot be expressed or are simply not true in the third person singular or plural, or in relation to a general subject ("one"), it indicates that the one who is in question here is not somebody, not "the people," but *I myself* in the strictest sense. These aphorisms, sharp not only in their content but also in their formulation, hence equally avoid the Scylla of theologico-philosophical terminology's dry objectivism, and the Charybdis of religious discourse's didactic moralism.

What András László represents, and what manifests in his words, is true esoterism. This is not because his style is enigmatic, or because he wraps his message in barely decipherable symbolic language, or because he discloses ancient Far-Eastern teachings kept secret for millennia—but because he formulates his thoughts on such a high intellectual and linguistic level that they are inevitably available only to the most superior readers. The quintessential knowledge contained in these maxims includes all that is worth knowing. Through the exceptional intensity of his writing, and via the illuminating power of his aphorisms, András László is able to illuminate such depths as had been obscured by the veil of darkness until now. His maxims have the power to inflame in the reader that level of understanding which belongs to the world of intuition. By the unusual weight of intellect manifesting in the flash of understanding, the appreciative reader is now bewildered, now mesmerized—and we know well from Plato that exactly this is the beginning of all true wisdom... Orientation: this is what András László offers. Absolute orientation! András László has imbibed the knowledge of the ancients, added his own wisdom, and distilled it until it is purified and condensed into these quintessential maxims. Those who have had the opportunity to survey the authors of those philosophical-spiritual works written in a similar vein and that deal with similar topics can testify that such essential and central knowledge as this can hardly be found anywhere else. All that is knowable and worth knowing in an essential sense can be found in these aphorisms. Together with Angelus Silesius, we can say that there is only one path leading us further:

> *It is enough now, my friend. If you would ask for more,*
> *go and become the Word and the Essence yourself.*

Ferenc Buji

Index

A

absolute, the, §§ 114, 133, 417, 657; absolute center, pp. 158-59; absolute omnipotence (*omnipotentia absoluta*), § 777; absolute omnipresence (*omnipresentia absoluta*), § 777; absolute omniscience (*omniscientia absoluta*), § 777; absolute realization, § 280; absolute subject, § 81
absolution, §§ 275, 582, 710; contrast: annihilation
abstraction, § 426; contrast: surpassing
ācārya, §§ 253-54, p. 9
acclimatization, § 376
action, §§ 91, 97, 169, 212, 228, 246, 273, 439, 636, 680, 682, pp. 139, 149; action and inaction, § 636; see also: *wei wu wei*
Adam (Biblical), § 731 n57; Adam Harisón, § 731 n57; Adam Qadmón, § 731
Adorno, Theodor, pp. 166, 168
advaita vedānta, p. 152

aggression, § 452
aham ātmā, § 714
Ahogy Lehet, § 252
albedo, §§ 605, 713
alétheia, §§ 732-33
alienation, §§ 105, 366; see also: person; personality
Alliance of Free Democrats, 510 n35
Alliance of Young Democrats, 510 n35
Alpha & Ómega, § 729
amalgamation, § 58; contrast: uniformity; unity
ambition, § 416
America, §§ 398, 464, 574; Native Americans, § 574; pre-Columbian, p. 140
anagogic & katagogic, § 479
anarchism, §§ 469-70, 492
anārya, § 340
ancestors, § 125
András László, §§ 167 n9, 281n17, 303 n21, 311 n23, 469 n29, 613 n47, 741 n60, pp. 9, 147, 150-152, 154, 157, 170-173, 197;
androgyne & androgynity, §§ 614, 618, 626-27, 651; hyper-androgyne, §

619; see also: dyogenity;
gynandromorphism
Angelus Silesius, p. 173
animism, p. 168; contrast:
industrialism
annihilation, §§ 287, 290
n19, 326 n24, 331, 515,
530, 557, 709-10, 738,
744-45; contrast: absolution
anti-ecclesiaticism, § 569
antihierarchy, §§ 318, 631;
contrast: hierarchy
antiquity, §§ 525, 530;
antitradition & antitraditionality, §§ 232, 300-06,
316, 322-23, 326, 341-42,
390, 447, 462, 468, 473,
528, 773, pp. 139, 142-43,
154; contrast: tradition;
traditionality
apodictic necessity; see: *necessarium apodicticum*
apoliticism, § 445, p. 169
archaic, culture, p. 157; documents, § 297; in time,
§§ 525, 662; languages, §
599; man, § 240, p. 145;
state of being, § 614, p.
145; understanding, §
736; world, p. 145
Arhats, p. 168
arhythmicity, § 316; contrast: rhythmicity

aristocratic, institutions, p.
163; spirit as, §§ 449-50;
caste § 667 n53
arkhé, §§ 662, 735n59
Árpád, House of, § 476
artifex, § 541
ārya, § 340
ascent, §§ 203-04, 241, 747;
contrast: descent; see
also: cycles
asceticism, §§ 242, 415
asexuality, § 620
asmitā, § 718
astitā § 718
Aszfaltútépítő Vállalat (Asphalt Road Construction
Company), p. 148
atheism & atheists, §§ 32,
397, 437, 438, 441, 566, p.
154; see also: materialism & materialists
ativarṇa brāhmaṇa, § 667
ātmā, § 81, p. 153; see also:
aham ātmā;
Austro-Hungarian Monarchy, § 464
automatism, § 163, 641
auton, §§ 83-85, 87, 111 n7,
295, p. 151; contrast:
heteron
autonomy, §§ 517, 520, 608
n46, 769; contrast: heteronomy
autotheism, p. 151

avarṇa, § 667
avatāra, § 619
avoluntaristic or antivoluntaristic state, § 779; contrast: Freedom
awakening, §§ 157, 222, 233, 236 n13, 259, 271, 275-76, 287, 290, 769, pp. 153, 169.
axiality, §§ 61, 727, p. 156; see also: Center; centrality

| B

bandha, § 246; see also: bondage
Barth, Karl, § 31 n1
beauty, §§ 74, 534, 542-43, p. 157
becoming, §§ 41, 82 n4, 214, 261, 270, 305, 308 n22, 326 n24, 613 n47, 620, 664, pp. 151, 154;
beginning, §§ 668, 720-22, 727-28, 730-33, 735-37, 739-41, 760, 763; p. 145, 154, 173
Being beyond Being, the, §§ 270, 721
Being, the §§ 13, 47, 51, 55, 61, 66, 81 n3, 100, 107, 244, 254, 270, 275, 278-80, 296, 378, 519, 551, 568, 582, 613 n47, 616, 661, 682, 721, 755, 758, pp. 149, 151, 153; law of, p. 153; order of, p. 143; see also: Being which is beyond Being, the
Being-concept, §8, p. 171
Being-contemplation, §8
bhāvacakra, § 613 n47
bisectedness, § 615
body, §§ 178, 439, 459, 679n54, 690-96, 698; skeleton as the most petrified part of, § 698
bondage, §§ 5, 161, 246; see also: *bandha*
brāhmaṇa, § 667
Budapest, pp. 147, 149
buddha, §§ 253, 278
Buddha, the, §§ 1, 592, 741n60, p. 168
Buddhism, §§ 551, 572, 652 n50, p. 149; Tibetan Tantric, § 613 n47
Buddhist Mission, p. 148
Buji, Ferenc, p. 10

| C

cakravartī, § 748; see also: Wheel of Becoming
Canada, p. 140
caste(s), §§ 340, 667; archcaste, § 667 n53; subcastes, § 667 n53
center, the, §§ 39, 40, 51, 201, 208, 217, 270, 274,

305, 327, 454-55, 500, 515, 660, 759, 772; p. 144; of Being, §§ 519, 661; of the Being beyond Being, §§ 270, 721; of consciousness, § 52; of the world of becoming, §§ 305, 765; see also: axiality; centrality; centripetal striving; *motor immobilis; Principium Principiorum;* contrast: periphery
centrality, §§ 30, 61, 727; see also: axiality; center
centrifugal drifting, p. 144; contrast: centripetal striving
centripetal striving, p. 144; contrast: centrifugal drifting
children, §§ 184-85, 504, 610, 631
Christ (Jesus), §§ 64, 234, 436
Christian-Democratic People's Party, 510 n35
Christianity, §§ 554-55, 572-74, 576, p. 149; Western, § 530; see also: tradition, Christian
chthonic, § 537
Church, §§ 303 n21, 570-71, pp. 163, 171
circum-centro-complexity, § 772
circumstances, §§ 193, 220, 245, 517, 587, 621, 688, p. 9, 141, 151, 170
civilization, §§ 526-27; pseudo-, § 527; secular, pp. 164; technical, § 668; technological, § 393
combat, §§ 632, 637
comfort, p. 143
Communism, §§ 469, 471-72, 538
comprehension, §§ 154, 649, 651, 655; intellectual, p. 152; compare: feeling
concentration, §§ 247-48, 643-44; see also: *dhāraṇā*
confession, § 527; pseudo-, § 527
conformity & conformisation, § 328
conquering the world, p. 143
consciousness, §§ 44, 52, 92-96, 111, 128, 139, 154, 163, 208, 211, 244, 313, 329, 341, 360, 365, 385, 432, 466, 502, 513, 551, 558, 564, 597, 613, 663-64, 670, 681, 690, 694, 704, 709, 713, 728, 740, p. 149; Center-consciousness, § 454; I-consciousness, § 667 n53
consumption, pp. 143, 156-

58, 162
contemplation, §§ 10-11, p. 150; see also: world-contemplation
contingencies, §§ 432, 466, 746
control, §§ 245-46, 288, 677, 742-44, pp. 164-65; of processes, p. 16; see also: self-control
cosmos, §§ 30, 112, 260, 283, 285, 677
createdness, §§ 103, 119; compare: creation
creation, §§ 135, 611; compare: createdness
creator, §§ 101, 119, 135, 210, 280; creatorness, § 103
crime, §§ 166, 167 n9, p. 157
crisis(es), and catastrophes, § 388; economic, § 538; of consciousness, p. 149; of the modern world, § 343, p. 149
culture, §§ 526-29, pp. 124, 131, 137; archaic-traditional, p. 157; collapse of, § 539; consumer-oriented, p. 156; counter-culture, §§ 528-29; destructive, p. 157; exalting, p. 157; mass, pp. 156-157; modern, § 528; normal function of, p. 157; post-modern, p. 157; preserving, p. 157; pseudo-, §§ 527-28; reflective, p. 157; secular, p. 164
cycle(s), §§ 514-15, 747, 759, pp. 145-46, 162; doctrine of, § 516; cyclicity, § 747
Czakó, Gábor, p. 168

D

damnation, § 710; compare: annihilation; contrast: salvation
dark age, §§ 364, 373, 391, 439, 454, 513, 568, 700, pp. 150, 154; see also: *kali yuga*
darkening, §§ 348, 360, 531, 553; Age of Darkening, § 522; Endarkening, § 533
darkness, §§ 131, 152, 161, 224, 253, 312, 319, 331, 333-35, 350, 355, 365, 375, 404-05, 407, 409, 480, 514, 528-29, 581, 632-34, 725, p. 173; rule of, §§ 312, 331; see also: devoured, being; scotasmocracy
death, §§ 139, 142, 191, 257, 607, 637, 698, 700, 704, 706-10, 723-25, p.148; angel of, §§ 698-99; conquering, § 637; death-

force(s), §§ 333, 343, 420
Debrecen, p. 149
decline, §§ 3, 105, 142, 146, 150, 352, 386, 394, 533, 672, 746, pp. 154, 164; see also: alienation; contrast: progress
degeneration, §§ 306, 356, 370, 386, 416, 509, 533, 652
demagogy, p. 160
democracy, §§ 163, 467-68, 499-500, 504, 506, 512, pp. 149, 160, 167-67; democratism, § 479, pp. 144, 160; social democracy, p. 162
demon(s) & the demonic, §§ 29, 351, 366, 371, 398, 536-37, 556, 750; contrast: divine, the
démos, § 502
descent, §§ 48, 146-47, 241, 288, 345, 386, 437, 598, 603, 619, 666, 747, pp. 154-56; contrast: ascent; see also: cycles
deterioration, §§ 185, 329, 377, 391, p. 154
deviation, §§ 183, 377, 396, 401; pseudo-esoteric, p. 171; spiritual, §§ 406, 422, p. 149
deviationology, § 396; contrast: paradoseology
Devil, §§ 251, 360, 423
devoured, being, §§ 331-32; see also: darkness, rule of
dhāraṇā, § 248; see also: concentration
dialogue, Catholic-Marxist, § 303 n21; with God, § 562
dictatorship, § 468; Communist, p. 160; of light, § 481
differentiation, §§ 33, 56, 60, 463, 518, p. 169; contrast, non-differentiation
dignity, §§ 441, 484, pp. 164, 168
disintegration, §§ 309, 313, 323, 333, 343, 374, 379, 381, 474, 518, 522, 603, 608 n46, 651, 758, pp. 144, 154, 160; of Tradition, pp. 158-59; of all values, p. 169
dissipation, § 377
diversity, p. 141; compare: unity
divine, the, § 556, pp. 158, 163; divine king of Rome, § 457; divine man, § 619; divine totality, § 326 n24; contrast: demons & the demonic

doing and non-doing, § 636
domination, §§ 452-53, 503,
    735, 740, 753, 774; compare: power; supremacy
dream, §§ 96, 102, 254, p.
    153; see also: dream
    world; illusion; *māyā*
dream-world, § 276 n16, p.
    153; contrast: waking
    world; see also: illusion;
    māyā
duality, §§ 581, 615, 649
duḥkha, § 652 n50
duty, §§ 610, 623; see also:
    man, mission of
dynamic, § 344, p. 145; contrast: static
dyogeneity, § 614; see also:
    androgyny; gynadromorphism

E

eclipse, § 603
economics, p. 162
egalitarianism, §§ 482, 484,
    486, 489, p. 161; see also:
    equality
ego, pp. 151, 169; egoism, pp.
    150-51
Egypt, § 116
election(s), §§ 505, 510 n35,
    p. 166-68
emotion, emotional, §§ 88
    n5, 306, 649, 652 n50,
    653-54, 689; emotionality, §§ 644, 651-52; supra-emotionality, § 655
enchantment, §§ 100, 103,
    123, p. 153; see also:
    magic
English Civil War, § 437
engrossment, § 226
Enlightenment, §§ 522,
    531-33
entertainment, p. 143
equality, §§ 318, 483, 487,
    489, p. 150
essentiality, § 665
eternal, §§ 34, 294, 604 n44,
    702, 721, 735, 761-62
eternity, §§ 457, 700, 761-63,
    765-66, 768, pp. 145, 149
ethics, §§ 580-87; moral
    commandment or rule,
    §§ 583-84
Éttermi és Büfé Vállalat (Catering and Buffet Company), p. 148
Europe, §§ 398, 464, pp. 9,
    150
evil, § 4
Evola, Julius, §§ 290 n19,
    390, p. 9, 166
evolution, evolutionism, §§
    318, 418, 494, 593-94,
    599, pp. 143, 154; see
    also: involution & evolution

Exodus, § 780
expansion, p. 143-44, 155
experience, §§ 59, 102, 108, 113, 116, 119, 126, 147, 170, 213, 263, 290 n14, 439, 518, 563, 593, 627, 700, 707, 712, 736, 757, p. 150; artistic, § 544; living, p. 152; self-experience, §§ 35, 111 n7; spiritual, § 212
experiencer, §§ 59-60, 212-13

F

faith, § 561, p. 149
fall, the, § 353
false rhetoric, §§ 21-23, 486
Far-Eastern religions, 308 n22, pp. 147; Westernized forms of, p. 171
fate, §§ 179, 192, 246
fear, § 287
feeling, §§ 127, 170, 172, 649-50, 651-53, 655
feminine, § 613 n47, p. 152
First World War, § 464
forces, of darkness, §§ 152, 333, 335, 365, 375; of light, §§ 152, 375; satanic, §§ 372, 410
freedom, §§ 168, 774, 776-77, 779, pp. 146, 149, 158, 163-69; of opinion, § 497; contrast: avoluntaristic or antivoluntaristic state; indetermination;
French Revolution, §§ 437, 523
functionalism, p. 143
future, §§ 754, 757-58

G

German Empire, § 464
global market, p. 143; globalism, p. 141
gnostic spirituality, pp. 146
goal, §§ 34, 141, 173-74, 197, 208-09, 218, 259, 264-65, 268, 283, 293, 428, 431, 568, 623, 779, pp. 143, 158, 161; ultimate, §§ 205, 210, 259, 283, 308 n22, 326 n23, 326 n24, p. 143; see also: Norm; Organizing Principle; Source
God, §§ 13, 21, 31, 69-75, 239, 326 n24, 341, 423, 438, 461, 511, 523, 543, 558-59, 562, 566, 600, 760, pp. 140, 143, 150-51, 154-55, 163, 167, 169; God-man, § 618
Golden Age, §§ 233, 373, 375, 395; contrast, *kali-yuga*
good, §§ 4, 167, 173, 339, 342, 351, 543
grace, § 563
Greece (modern), p. 140
Greek mythology, § 732 n58

Guénon, René, §§ 343, 390, 678, pp. 9, 142
guru(s), iii, §§ 253, 256, 402; pseudo-*gurus*, § 410; see also: master & disciple; masters
gynandromorphism, § 614; see also: androgyny; dyogeneity

H

Hades, § 732 n58
Hamvas, Béla, pp. 148, 155
Hayek, Friedrich A., p. 162
Heaven, §§ 62, 204, 234, 283, 341, 607, p. 163
Hegel, G. W. F., § 764
Heidegger, Martin, § 390
Heisenberg, Werner, p. 155
heresy, §§ 546, 572
heteron, §§ 83-90, 111 n7, 221, 651, 774, pp. 151, 153; contrast: *auton*
heteronomy, § 131; contrast: autonomy
hierarchical grades or levels, §§ 33, 463, 585, 605 n45, 664, 695, 761; structures, p. 158
hierarchy, §§ 660, 664; feudal, § 461; of castes, § 667; of consciousness, § 670; of the order of Being, p. 143; contrast:

antihierarchy
historicity, §§ 518-19, 521, 614, pp. 145, 149; sub-historicity, §§ 518, 520, 614, p. 149; supra-historicity, § 518, p. 149
history, §§ 517, 521-22, 524, pp. 140, 150, 154, 159, 161; celestial § 517; mythical, § 517; prehistory, p. 140; posthistory, p. 140; transcendent, § 517; see also: ascent; descent; historicity
Homo religiosus, p. 146
homunculi, p. 167
honesty, § 349
honor, § 349
horizontalism, pp. 142-44; contrast: verticalism
humanism, §§ 318, 428-31, pp. 143, 155, 160
humanitarian, § 431
Hungarian Democratic Forum, § 510 n35
Hungarian Revolution (1848), § 473 n30
Hungary, § 473 n30, pp. 9, 148, 169
hypercosmia, § 30

I

I myself, §§ 76, 81 n3, 106-07, 114, 121, 156, 222, 271, 646,

714-15, 737, 775, 779, pp.
150, 172; I-myselfness,
§ 127; compare: Myself;
own person; contrast:
psychological I-ness
idealism, extreme, § 432;
subjective, § 82 n4
identification, §§ 113, 122,
207, 268, 290, 709, 717,
pp. 151, 153, 166; absolute, § 205; individual,
326 n24; personal, §
205; self-identification,
§ 55
ignorance, § 533 n37
illusion, §§ 78, 99, pp. 167,
169; see also: dream;
dream-world; *māyā*
immanence, §§ 45, 541, 552;
immortality, §§ 711-12, p.
149; absolute, § 722; relative, § 713
incarnation, §§ 118, 120, 284
n18, 419; reincarnation, §
419, p 169
indetermination, § 779; contrast: freedom
India, §§ 254, 340 n25, 398
Individuum Absolutum, § 267,
p. 150; contrast: *individuum isolatum;*
individuum isolatum § 267;
contrast: *Individuum Absolutum*

industrialism, p. 168; contrast: animism
inertia, p. 163-65, 168,
infinity, §§ 79, 111, 712, 764;
Hegel's "bad infinity," §
764
initiation, §§ 189, 196, 340
n25, 399-400, 413; initiate(s), §§ 235-36, 240;
modern man as uninitiable, §§ 235, 240; pseudo and counter-, § 400
instinct(s), §§ 168, 622, 751,
769, p. 157; contrast:
volition
Institute of Buddhology, p.
148
instrumentalism, p. 143
intellect, intellectual, §§
229, 641, pp. 139, 147, 152,
161, 171, 173
internationalism, §§ 473,
477-78, p. 160; contrast:
nationalism
intuition, § 54, 248, 646-48,
650, 655, p. 173;
involution & evolution, §§
593-603; see also: evolution
Iupiter Stator, §§ 456-57

J

Jacob's Ladder, § 204
journalism, § 372

K

kali-yuga, §§ 233, 324, 329-30, 332, 341, 346, 359, 374-75, 387, 517, 553, pp. 10, 150, 154, 162; see also: dark age
karma, § 246;
Kerényi, Carl, § 26
king, §§ 457, 476, 500, 686, pp. 151, 163; see also: monarch
Kőrösi Csoma Sándor Buddhist Seminary, p. 148
kṣatriya, §§ 340 n25, 667

L

laissez faire, p. 162
language(s), § 599; as a tradition, § 300; theological, 562; symbolic, p. 173
last man, p. 161
Leftism, §§ 446-47, 470, 473, pp. 158-160, 162, 170; leftward drift, p. 158; contrast: Rightism
Léthé, § 732 n58
level(s), cultural, p. 156; cosmic, § 260; existential, §§ 53, 391, pp. 156, 162; hierarchical, §§ 33, 585; human, §§ 431, 620; linguistic, p. 173; of a category's basic elements, § 475; of an avatāra, § 619; of blood ties, § 474; of the demands of mass culture, p. 131; of religion, § 710 p. 161; of systems, § 770; of the Earth, § 234; of the world of becoming, 82 n4; of truth, § 669; of understanding, p. 147; psychological, p. 162; social, p. 160
liberalism, §§ 469, 487-88, 490, 494, 498, pp. 149, 161-62; anti-liberalism, §§ 490, 492; liberality, §§ 492, 494; liberal(s), §§ 491-92, pp. 165-67
liberation (mere *emantipatio*), p. 165; spiritual, § 290 n19
libertas, § 494
life, §§ 22, 32, 132-33, 139, 141-42, 147, 149, 182, 197, 215-16, 223-24, 227, 257, 282, 314-16, 334, 425, 463, 486, 585, 620, 625-26, 631, 652, 689, 700, 705-08, pp. 9, 140, 143, 147, 158, 163, 166, 172; beyond life, §§ 141, 708; supra-life, § 568
light, §§ 239, 350, 514, 528, 581, 725, 761; dictatorship of, § 481; forces of,

§§ 152, 375, 409, 501, 529, 632; inner, § 582; light-like, § 635; of consciousness, § 681; *The Light of the All in Man*, p. 148; of the world, § 64; victory of, § 480
logic, logical, §§ 13, 484, pp. 151, 154;
Logos, the, § 564, p. 149
lunar, §§ 179, 667

M

machines, § 366
magic, § 103; magician, 104; see also: enchantment
mahāyuga, § 514
man and woman, §§ 614, 629, 651; see also: man; woman
man, §§ 118-131, *et passim;* ancient man, pp. 139, 140, 146, 147, 158, 170; archaic, § 240, pp. 145; cosmic man, § 595; mass-man, 166; mission of, § 623; modern man, 235, 240, 326, 601, 701, p. 145, 155, 157, 162, 166; personal man, § 126; spiritual man, § 216, 232, 700; Universal Man, §§ 120, 284 n18, 595; see also: man and woman; duty

mania, § 164
Māra, § 572
marriage, §§ 607, 627
Marxism, §§ 303 n21, 440; see also: post-Marxist worldview; socialism
masculine, § 613 n47, p. 152
mask (*persona*), §§ 115, 124
mass communication, § 5
masses, pp. 146, 163, 164, 165, 166,
master & disciple, §§ 253-56; see also: gurus; masters, spiritual masters, Eastern, § 255; spiritual, iii, § 410; see also: gurus; master & disciple
materialism & materialists, §§ 10, 82 n4, 343, 397, 398, 432-36, 438, 441, 533, 547, 607, p. 162; see also: atheism materialization, §§ 595, 597
māyā, § 100, p. 153; see also: dream; dream world; illusion
mediocrity, §§ 152-53
meditation, §§ 247, 414, p. 170
Meister Eckhart, p. 150
messianism, p. 161
metaphysica traditionalis, p. 147
metaphysica vera, § 526, p. 147

metaphysical praxis, p. 149
metaphysical tradition(ality), §§ 13, 34, 36, 293, 295, 480, 526 n56, 557, 571, 593, 742, pp. 139, 140, 146, 147, 149
metaphysical vision, §§ 53, 63
metaphysics, §§ 35, 37, 38, 43, 296, p. 145, 147, 171; of sexuality, p. 149; traditional, p. 146
Metaphysicum Absolutum, §§ 68, 82 n4, 290 n19, pp. 140, 154; contrast: *Individuum Absolutum*
metapolitics, § 445
Middle Ages, § 522
miracles, §§ 157, 362, 390
missionaries, § 574
modern world, §§ 232, 319, 343, 362, 376, 399, 570, pp. 140-44; see also: modern worldview; modernity
modernity, §§ 233 n11, 298, 315, 321-22, 325, 327-28, 344, 347, 379-80, 526, pp. 139-43; see also: modern world; modern worldview
monarch, § 455
monarchy, §§ 453, 458, 479 n32, 686; constitutional, § 466; see also: king
money, § 370
Morris, Desmond, § 598 n43, *The Human Animal*, 598 n43; *The Naked Ape*, 598 n43
Mors triumphalis, § 637
motor immobilis, p. 144; see also: Center
music, § 341, Negroid, § 537; popular, 535-36
Myself, §§ 71, 77, 114, 117, 239, 265, 269, 271, 600, 733, pp. 150, 153
myselfness, §§ 116, 127; see also: I myself
mysteries (religious), §§ 399, 401

N

Nagycenk, p. 149
narcissism, social, p. 160
Nasafī, 'Azīz, p. 151
nationalism, §§ 473, 474 n31, 477-78, p. 160; contrast: internationalism
natural, §§ 361, 424, 427, p. 162; contrast: supernatural
nature (essence), §§ 10, 65, 108, 119, 320, 326 n24, 351, 408, 435, 437, 457, 542, 641 n48, 750, 767, 771, p. 141, 142, 150, 160,

161, 165, 168
nature (realm), §§ 315, 341, 424-27
necessarium apodicticum, § 67
neglect, §§ 754-55
Neoplatonism, p. 152
New Age-type "esoteric spirituality," p. 171
nigredo, §§ 605, 713
nirguṇa mūla prakṛti, §§ 326 n24, § 675
nirvāṇa, §§ 50, 281, 282, 592
noble, p. 157
non-differentiation, § 56; contrast: differentiation; compare: undifferentiationism
Norm, pp. 143, 154; see also: Goal; Organizing Principle; Source
normality, § 39, p. 142
North Pole, p. 155-56
North Star, p. 156
nothingness, §§ 90, 97, 133, 191, 377, p. 155
Nyíregyháza, p. 149

O

Objectivism, §§ 434, 442-44, p. 172
objectivity, §§ 69, 92
occultisms, § 418
Order, §§ 769-73, pp. 158, 163-65; counter-order, p. 160; dark order of things, § 310; of Being, p. 143; of the spirit, § 216; of values, pp. 139-40; contrast: Freedom
organic, order, §§ 770-71; substance, § 631
Organizing Principle, p. 143; compare: Goal; Norm; Source
orgasm, § 628
orientation, §§ 159, 724, pp. 149, 162, 171; spiritual, p. 171
origin, §§ 47, 61, 192, 208, 293, 298, 308 n22, 668, 727, 733-34, 773; extra*saṁsāra*ic, 61, 667 n53; heavenly, § 295; hypercosmic, § 595; metaphysical, p. 149; of being, § 426; of man, §§ 424, 428; Negroid, § 537; primordial, § 540
origin-awareness, §§ 734, 738, 740
Ortega y Gasset, José, pp. 163, 172
own person, pp. 152-53; see also: Myself; I myself; Universal Subject

P

pacificist, § 639
pañcaka, § 667
Parable of Talents, p. 172
paradoseology, § 396; contrast: deviationology
parents, § 610
Paris Commune, § 438 n28
past, §§ 178, 189-90, 402, 754-58, pp. 140-41, 154, 157, 166
path, §§ 268, 293; cosmic, § 595; downward, § 187; from forms and consciousness to transcendence, § 664; from suprahistoricity through historicity towards sub-historicity, p. 149; from transcendence to the world, § 664; in arts, § 540; metaphysical, p. 152; narrow, § 191; of gradual materialization, § 595; of least resistance, p. 171; of realization, § 285; of surpassing temporality, § 767; of Tantric-yoga, §§ 624-25; spiritual, §§ 191, 199, 230, 270, 399, 421, pp. 158, 170; to chaos, § 310; to myself, 38, 117, 209, 215; to supra-topical thinking, § 645; wayless, § 191; wide, § 191; wrong, §§ 141, 144
pax post victoriam lucis & tenebrarum § 480
peace, §§ 480, 639
perception, §§ 101, 130, 443
perennitas, §§ 761-62
perfection, §§ 97, 142
periphery, §§ 40, 51, 217, 274, 500, p. 144; see also: centrifugal drifting; contrast: Center, the
person, §§ 81 n3, 112-13, 115, 117, 207, 214, 285, 568, 715, p. 152-53; contrast: Subject; see also: own person
personality, 9, §§ 105-06, 111, 283, 452, 721; contrast: Subject; see also: alienation; person
pessimism, § 705
Petőfi, Sándor, § 473 n28
philosophers & philosophy, §§ 577-80
philosophia perennis, §§ 577, 763
Physicum Nihilum, p. 155
piecework, § 371; contrast: time wage
pistis, § 286
Plato, §§ 533; p. 151, 160, 166, 173; *Laws*, § 533 n37

pneumatosis, §§ 391-92, 684-85
polar, §§ 295, 667; compare: solar
polarity, §§ 61, 667n53
politics, §§ 445-481, 499, pp. 158, 167, 169
polygamy, §§ 608-09
pontifex, § 541
populism, p. 160
post-Marxism §§ 383-385
postmodernity, §§ 379-83
potentia passiva pura, § 675
potentiality, §§ 326 n24, 674, 758
power, §§ 164, 219, 222, 279, 335, 362, 370, 432, 439, 452-53, 460, 558, 563, 613, 667 n53, 749, 774, pp. 164-69; compare: domination; supremacy
pragmatism, p. 143
pralaya, § 387
praxis, §§ 409-10, pp. 149, 154
prayer, § 559-60
predestination, § 778
preparation, §§ 189, 429, 506, p. 144
present, §§ 338, 342, 508, 754-58, 767-68; present age, § 17, 375; present historical moment, p. 169; present world, §§ 337, 342-43, 467, p. 139
prima materia, § 675
Principium Principiorum, pp. 144, 163
Principium, § 735 n59
principles, §§ 11, 136, 140, 291, 317, 490, pp. 140-42, 144, 155, 158, 163; divine, p. 158; of modernity, pp. 142, 144; of traditionality, 142; supra-human, § 140
problem-solving, § 642
profit, p. 143
progress, §§ 594, 601, pp. 154-55; social, p. 143; spiritual, § 229; contrast: decline
Protestantism, § 437
prudence, § 349
psychological I-ness, § 127; contrast: I-myselfness
psychological level, §§ 162, 612, p. 162
psychological typologies, p. 168; contrast: qualitative typologies
psychology, § 550, p. 162
psychosis, § 391, 392
Purgatory, § 283

Q

qualitative typologies, p. 168; contrast: psycholog-

ical typologies
quality, §§ 487-88, 671-77, p. 156; of being, § 222; quality–quantity reciprocity, p. 171; contrast: quantity
quantitative, aspects, §§ 672-73, 678, pp. 141, 156; world, §§ 394, 696
quantity, §§ 671-77, p. 160; of time, 371; quality–quantity reciprocity, p. 171; contrast: quality

R

Ramaṇa Maharṣi (Bhagavān Śrī), p. 9, § 247, pp. 151, 170
rationalism, §§ 364, 580, p. 161
reality, §§ 12, 65, 95, 99, 100, 111n7, 344, 426, 589, 619, 690, 727, 740, p. 152; objective, §§ 93-96; ontological, 612; subjective, 93
realization, §§ 13, 36, 37, 71, 129, 188, 189, 199, 208, 212, 214, 242, 250, 257, 260, 261, 266, 270, 272-74, 280, 284-86, 288-89, 308 n22, 325, 568, 582, 656, 726, 764; metaphysical, §§ 188-89, 260, 284

recollection, metaphysical, § 298; ontological, § 734
Reformation, § 575
relativism, pp. 142, 143, 161
religio perennis, §§ 762 n64, 763
religion, §§ 527, 551-68; pp. 146, 148, 149, 161, 162; Christian, § 572; counter-, § 441; perennial, § 763; philosophy of, p. 148; pseudo-, § 527; state, § 441; unlike metaphysics, § 43; see also: religiosity
religiosity, mass, p. 146; of ancient man, p. 146; of today's man, 145; pseudo-, 146; self-service, p. 161
Renaissance, §§ 522, 530
repression, p. 162
reproduction, § 617
restoration, inner, § 563; of the body, § 695; of unity, § 611, 616-17, 626
resurrection, §§ 694-95
return, to non-oblivion, § 734; to Oneself, § 215, p. 153; to the origin, §§ 192, 773; to the spirit, § 190
revolt, §§ 153, 179, 750
revolutionary ideology, p. 161

revolutionary violence, pp. 161, 168
rhythmicity, § 227; contrast: arrhythmicity
riding the tiger, § 308
Rightism or Right-wing, §§ 447-48, 451, 462, 477, 491 n33, pp. 149, 150, 158-160; always theocratic, p. 163; extreme, p. 160; maximal, pp. 160, 162; Parliamentary, p 159; contrast: Leftism
Rome, § 457
rubedo, §§ 605, 713
Russian Revolution, § 437
Russian Tsarist Empire, § 464

S

salvation, §§ 236 n13, 259, 710; compare: absolution; contrast: damnation
saṁsāra, §§ 50, 61, 295, 558, 591, 592, 667 n53, pp. 156, 161
satanicity, § 409
Schuon, Frithjof, p. 9
science, §§ 546-50, pp. 143, 149, 155
scotasmocracy, §§ 311-12, 510; see also: darkness, rule of

Second World War, § 464
Self, § 632; actual, p. 151; suprapersonal, § 324; true, p. 151; ultimate, § 207, p. 151; see also: self-realization
self-control, §§ 163, 166, 167 n9, 688, p. 164; see also: control
self-denial (negative), § 367
self-identify, § 55, 290 n19; see also: identification
selfishness, § 171; unselfishness, p. 151
self-overcoming, p. 172
self-realization, §§ 270, 568, 582; see also: Self
sensation, § 652
sensus, §§ 649, 651
sentimentality, § 412, pp. 157, 171
sexes, differences between, §§ 614, 630-31; see also: androgyne & androgyny
sexuality, §§ 308 n22, 612, 615-17, 621, 625-26, p. 149
shamanism & shamans, § 554-55
Śikhidhvaja, p. 151
sin, §§ 166-67, 573, 579, 586, p. 157
skeleton, §§ 698-99
slavery, pp. 166-67
socialism, § 440, p. 143,

160; see also: Marxism; post-Marxist worldview
solar, §§ 295, 667; compare: polar
solipsism & solipsists, §§ 21, 81, 82, pp. 150-52; metaphysical, §§ 81 n3, p. 125, 127; philosophical. p. 152
somatosis, §§ 391, 392
sophia perennis, § 763,
Sophia, § 604, p. 149
Sopron, p. 149
soul, §§ 109, 319, 335, 633, 652, 679 n54, 684, 686-89, 693, 696, p. 168
Source, the, §§ 238-39, 326, pp. 143-44, 154; see also: Goal, Norm
South Korea, p. 140
sovereignty, §§ 269, 736; popular, § 507, p. 160
space travel, p. 143
space, p. 9.
speed, p. 145
spirit, §§ 64, 109, 190, 216, 223, 237, 420, 426, 449-50, 468, 481, 499, 512, 531, 556, 602, 619, 663, 679-84, 686-89, 691-94, 696, 769, pp. 141, 169, 171; aristocratic, §§ 449-50, p. 163; autocratic, § 450; theocratic, § 450
spiritism, § 417

spiritual elite, § 285, p. 171
spirituality, §§ 31, 216, 355, 367, 422, 465, 764, pp. 145, 147, 158, 169, 170; and the intellect, pp. 147, 171; anti-, § 528; consumer-, p. 170; distorted, p. 146; gnostic, p. 146; modern, p. 169; of ancient man, p. 146; pseudo-, §§ 401, 408, 411, 421, 493 n34, p. 170
spontaneity, § 228, p. 158
sport, pp. 143, 168
stagnation, §§ 145-48
State (political), §§ 457-58, 460, pp. 149, 163; as a living organism, §§ 458, 460
states, ecstatic, § 537; manifested, § 238; of consciousness, §§ 513, 663, 690; of enchantment, §§ 100, 123; of the Being, §§ 55, 417; of self-identification, § 55; ordered, § 773; psychological, § 162
static, reality, § 344; versus dynamic, p. 145
Steffens, Heinrich, § 596
Stoicism, p. 168
subhuman, §§ 138, 140, 429
Subject, the, §§ 43, 79, 85, 107-110, 112, 115, 207, 211,

272-73, 285, 680, 682, 721, 729, pp. 150, 153; Absolute, § 81; Universal, §§ 76-82, p. 152; see also: I myself; Myself; Universal Subject; contrast: person; personality
subject-bearer, §§ 108, 111
subterrestrial, § 667
śūdra, § 667
superhuman, § 425
superiority, §§ 341, 452, 498, 507, 600-01, 663, 668, pp. 139, 154, 168
supernatural, §§ 361, 425, 427; contrast: natural
superstitions, §§ 318, 594
suprahuman, §§ 140, 413, 417, 428
suprapersonal, §§ 214, 324
supremacy, §§ 452-53; compare: domination, power
Supreme Being, § 523
surpassing, §§ 104, 426, 767, pp. 139, 165, 168-69, 172; contrast: abstraction
Svadharma, §§ 214-15
symbol(s), §§ 308 n22, 326 n24, 588 n41, 590, pp. 144-45
symbology, §§ 588-92; doctrinal, § 297
Szentendre, p. 149

T

technology, §§ 367, 393, 600, 602, pp. 143, 155
Teilhard de Chardin, Pierre, § 31 n1
temporality, §§ 292, 665, 757, 767, p. 139; see also: time
terrestrial, caste, § 667; Order, p. 158
terrorism, §§ 164, 468, 498; Bolshevist, 441, 467
theocratic, state, p. 163; spirit, § 450
theology, §§ 565, 569, pp. 123-24; Calvinist, pp. 147-48; Catholic, p. 148
theomonism, p. 151
thinking, §§ 443, 640, 642-45, pp. 139, 171; contrast: intuition
Tibet, § 398, p. 140
time wage, § 371; contrast: piecework
time, §§ 291, 525, 665, 754-69, pp. 145, 149; linear, p. 145; see also: temporality
totalitarianism, § 479
totemism, § 556
Tower of Babel, § 204
traditio perennis, § 762 n64
tradition, §§ 291-2, 294, 297-98, 300-02, 396, 527, 571, 576, 762n62, p. 139, 142-43, 147, 154-56,

158-59, 163; Catholic, § 607; in Christianity, § 571, 576; disintegration of, pp. 158-59; Hebrew, § 731 n57; Hindu, § 439; metaphysical, § 13, 293, 295, 480, 557, pp. 143, 154; primordial, § 296; Tantric, § 308 n22; universal, p. 149

traditional school, pp. 139, 140, 147, 155; of Hungary, p. 148;

traditional view, §§ 167 n9, 219, pp. 139, 144

traditional world, §§ 167 n9, 343, pp. 115-18, 164; see also: traditional worldview; contrast: modern world; modernity

traditionality, §§ 301, 303, 390, 447, 448, 464, 530, pp. 140-42, 144, 146-47, 149, 158, 164, 171; metaphysical, §§ 34, 36, 526 n36, 571, 593, 742, p. 139, 146-47; versus Modernity, pp. 140-47

transcendence, §§ 341, 541, 664, p. 146; self-transcendence, p. 158; contrast: immanence

transmutation, §§ 187, 267, 415, p. 149; of the Being,

§§ 8, 280

truth, §§ 172, 539, 589, 669, 732, p. 146, 151, 161; highest, 21; of solipsism, § 21; of Tradition, p. 139

Turkish Sultanate, § 464

Turuls, § 476

U

unbegun(ness), §§ 668, 722, 727, 733

unconscious, the, § 128

understanding, §§ 156, 650-51, 659, 683, 712, 736, p. 173

undifferentiationism, p. 169; compare: nondifferentiation

uniformity, p. 141; contrast: amalgamation; unity

unity, §§ 58, 97, 272, 274, 518, 564, 581, 611, 614, 616, 617, 650, 651, pp. 141-42, 144; compare: diversity; contrast, amalgamation; uniformity

Universal Subject, §§ 76-82, pp. 150, 152

unselfishness, p. 151

utopianism, p. 161

V

vaiśya, §§ 340 n25, 667

vajrayāna, p. 152

values, § 374-75, 529, 539,
　　pp. 139, 140, 157, 160-62,
　　169; counter-values, 157
verticalism, pp. 142-44;
　　contrast: horizontalism
victor, p. 164
victory, §§ 351, 480, 637, p.
　　165
vidyā, § 53
virginity, § 620
volition, §§ 241, 595, 622,
　　724, 743, 751; contrast:
　　instinct
vulgar, § 231, pp. 168-69
vulgarization, pp. 146, 169

About András László

András László (1941–2024) was born in Budapest. A revered teacher and prolific author, András László held a doctorate in Buddhist studies and was a leading exponent of the Hungarian Traditionalist school. His books include *A mindenség fénye az emberben* (*The Light of the Universe in Man*, 1965); *Tradicionalitás és létszemlélet* (*Tradition and Existence*, 1995); *Kard, kereszt, korona. Tradicionális tanulmányok a Magyarságról* (*Sword, Cross, Crown: Traditional Studies on Hungarianness* with Tibor Baranyi and Róbert Horváth, 2000); *Tradíció és metafizika. Kérdések és válaszok* (*Tradition and Metaphysics: Questions and Answers*, with Róbert Horváth, 2007); and *A jobboldaliság alapelvei* (*Principles of the Right*, 2013).

www.ingramcontent.com/pod-product-compliance
Lightning Source LLC
Chambersburg PA
CBHW030855170426
43193CB00009BA/623